Thriving in Grace

Thriving in Grace

Twelve Ways the Puritans Fuel Spiritual Growth

Joel R. Beeke
and
Brian G. Hedges

Reformation Heritage Books
Grand Rapids, Michigan

Thriving in Grace
© 2020 by Joel R. Beeke and Brian G. Hedges

Reformation Heritage Books
3070 29th St. SE
Grand Rapids, MI 49512
616-977-0889
orders@heritagebooks.org
www.heritagebooks.org

Printed in the United States of America
25 26 27 28 29/11 10 9 8 7 6 5 4 3

Library of Congress Cataloging-in-Publication Data

Names: Beeke, Joel R., 1952- author. | Hedges, Brian G., author.
Title: Thriving in grace : twelve ways the Puritans fuel spiritual growth /
    Joel R. Beeke and Brian G. Hedges.
Description: Grand Rapids, Michigan : Reformation Heritage Books, 2020. |
    Includes bibliographical references.
Identifiers: LCCN 2020014604 (print) | LCCN 2020014605 (ebook) |
    ISBN 9781601787842 (paperback) | ISBN 9781601787859 (epub)
Subjects: LCSH: Christian life—Puritan authors. | Puritans—Doctrines. |
    English literature—Puritan authors—History and criticism. | American
    literature—Puritan authors—History and criticism.
Classification: LCC BX9323 .B446 2020 (print) | LCC BX9323 (ebook) |
    DDC 248.4/859—dc23
LC record available at https://lccn.loc.gov/2020014604
LC ebook record available at https://lccn.loc.gov/2020014605

For
Ian Hamilton
a lover of our rich Puritan experiential heritage,
a treasured brother and warm friend and preacher,
whose every message enlightens my mind and feeds my soul.
"I thank my God upon every remembrance of you" (Philippians 1:3).

—JRB

&

Luke Potter
faithful brother and fellow laborer;
may the old Puritan motto,
Vincit Qui Patitur ("He who suffers conquers"),
always be inscribed on your heart, as you
"endure hardness as a good soldier of Jesus Christ" (2 Timothy 2:3).

—BGH

Table of Contents

Acknowledgments

When I consider the vast mines of rich Puritan literature available to us today, I vacillate between feeling like a kid in a candy store and being overwhelmed with "so many books, so little time!" Though I will never be able to read them all, I am deeply grateful for publishers like Banner of Truth and Reformation Heritage Books that have made so many of these books available and accessible to ordinary pastors like me. I read the Puritans because they feed my soul.

I also wish to thank the elders and members of Redeemer Church, who generously encourage me to devote time to reading and writing for the sake of the wider church, and also my beautiful wife, Holly, and our four kids, who never seem to begrudge the many hours spent in writing a new book.

Finally, I am grateful for Dr. Joel R. Beeke, who not only took an interest in my original proposal for this book, but was also willing to partner with me in contributing half its content. I've learned much from Dr. Beeke's expertise in Puritan literature and will continue to benefit from his scholarship, as well as his godly example, in the years to come.
—Brian G. Hedges

I wish to express my gratitude to Brian Hedges for a great working relationship. When he proposed a manuscript to Reformation Heritage Books of several chapters of this book, the Manuscript

Committee decided that it would be good if I were to join him as co-author in enlarging the book to twelve chapters, providing he was willing. Happily, he was more than willing! After collaborating on twelve subjects out of numerous possibilities, we decided to take responsibility for six chapters each; and Brian wrote the introduction and chapters 2, 4–6, and 9–10, while I wrote chapters 1, 3, 7–8, 11–12, and the conclusion. We then edited each other's chapters. Since we were responsible for writing different chapters, we chose, for the most part, to use singular pronouns rather than plural, on the infrequent occasions when we referred to our own thoughts and convictions. I found Brian to be a like-minded brother on his view of and love for Puritan authors, as well as a joy to work with and a good writer.

For the last 50+ years I have always tried to be reading at least one Puritan book. Many times I have thanked God for writers like Thomas Watson, John Bunyan, Thomas Brooks, Thomas Goodwin, and Anthony Burgess—each of which have been my favorite Puritan writer at different periods of my life. Over the decades, I have often felt like Luther when he said that most of his best friends were "dead ones"—sitting on his shelves. I cannot thank God's grace enough in raising up the Puritans to feed my soul like no other group of writers in church history.

I wish to express heartfelt gratitude to my special wife, Mary, who willingly gives me time and space to engage in a writing ministry—a ministry that I have felt called to since a teenager. As I often feel closest to God when I write, having a loving and understanding wife like her is an unspeakable treasure. Thanks, too, to Josef Urban for ably assisting me and adapting some of my former work for this book and to Ray Lanning for his faithful editing work. And thanks again to our faithful typesetter/proofreading team, Gary and Linda den Hollander, for their fine work.

We pray God that this little book will whet your appetite for reading the Puritans. If you want to know God and your own soul better, read the Puritans. You will not be sorry! By the Spirit's grace, you will "thrive in grace."

—Joel R. Beeke

Introduction

It is a sad fact that sometimes pediatricians diagnose children with a condition called FTT ("failure to thrive") syndrome.[1] The causes of FTT are many and varied, including genetics, sickness, and poor nutrition. But the diagnosis itself is given in cases of arrested development—when a child's growth measurements fall below a certain level or norm.

A similar condition is found in many Christians: spiritual FTT. Rather than abounding in love (1 Thess. 3:12), knowing the peace that passes all understanding (Phil. 4:7), and rejoicing with "joy unspeakable and full of glory" (1 Peter 1:8), these believers are marked by inconsistent and unhealthy patterns of growth and regression.

They languish in zeal and falter in hope. Their love for others sputters along, but rarely shifts into the higher gears of sacrificial generosity or service. While they have the capacity to feed on God's Word, they have to be spoon-fed. Their faith is weak, their hope burns dim, and the winds of adversity easily capsize and sink

---

1. Parts of this introduction are adapted from Brian G. Hedges, "Eight Road-blocks to Spiritual Health," first published online by Desiring God. See https://www.desiringgod.org/articles/eight-roadblocks-to-spiritual-health, accessed March 5, 2020.

their joy. These are cases of spiritual arrested development. Maybe this sounds like you.

As believers in Christ, we are commanded to grow in grace (2 Peter 3:18). In those soul-stirring words of Philip Bliss (1838–1876), we do well to cry from our hearts:

> More holiness give me,
> More sweetness within,
> More patience in suff'ring,
> More sorrow for sin;
> More faith in my Saviour,
> More sense of His care;
> More joy in His service,
> More purpose in prayer.[2]

But while we long for these "religious affections," as Jonathan Edwards called them, we often fail to thrive in them. Our motivational reach exceeds our practical grasp. Rather than grow and flourish, we struggle to keep our heads above water.

But this need not be so. It is possible for believers to not only get by but to grow and flourish in spiritual experience. And it is our conviction that few things could better facilitate such growth than a fresh reading of the English Puritans of the sixteenth and seventeenth centuries.[3]

Commenting on Peter's command to "grow in grace, and in the knowledge of our Lord and Savior Jesus Christ" (2 Peter 3:18),

---

2. P. P. Bliss, "My Prayer," No. 594, Stanza 1, *Gospel Hymns Nos. 1 to 6 Complete* (Bryn Mawr, Pa.: John Church Company: 1894).

3. For a helpful historical introduction to the Puritans, see Leland Ryken, *Worldly Saints: The Puritans As They Really Were* (Grand Rapids: Zondervan, 1990). The term "Puritan," though originally derogatory, in this book is a short-hand reference for that Reformed stream of theologians, pastors, and preachers in England, Scotland, and New England who ministered from the mid-sixteenth century to the late-seventeenth century—or, in the case of Jonathan Edwards in New England, into the eighteenth century. When referring to specific people from church history, our practice is to provide the dates of their lives in parentheses following their first reference in this book.

John Owen (1616–1683) observed that "it is not enough that we decay not in our spiritual condition"—we are also required to "endeavour after an improvement, an increase, a thriving in grace, that is, in holiness."[4] "Thriving in grace" is a beautiful description of gospel holiness and spiritual maturity.

The purpose of this book is to help believers thrive in grace through reading the Puritans. In the chapters that follow, we will explore twelve ways the Puritans can fuel our spiritual growth. Our sincere prayer is that reading these reflections will encourage you in your ongoing pursuit of, conformity to, and communion with, our Lord and Savior, Jesus Christ.

---

4. John Owen, *Pneumatologia, or A Discourse Concerning the Holy Spirit*, in *The Works of John Owen,* ed. W. H. Goold (1850–1853; repr., Edinburgh: Banner of Truth, 1966), 3:387.

—1—

THE PURITANS
Shape Our Lives by the
Authoritative Scriptures

The reading of the word is an ordinance of God, and mean[s] of salva-
tion, of God's own appointment. The Bible is this word, and God has
given it to us, and appointed it to be read.

—THOMAS BOSTON[1]

In John Bunyan's (1628–1688) famed *Pilgrim's Progress*, Christian is
escorted into a private room in the Interpreter's House. The Interpreter shows him a painting of metaphorical meaning: "Christian
saw the picture of a very grave person hang up against the wall; and
this was the fashion of it. It had eyes lifted up to Heaven, the best
of books in his hand, the law of truth was written upon his lips,
the world was behind his back. It stood as if it pleaded with men,
and a crown of gold did hang over its head."[2]

After explaining the meaning of the portrait, Interpreter said,
"I have showed thee this picture first, because the man whose picture this is, is the only man whom the Lord of the place whither
thou art going, hath authorized to be thy guide in all difficult

---

1. Thomas Boston, *An Illustration of the Doctrines of the Christian Religion*, in
The Whole Works of Thomas Boston, Part 2, ed. Samuel M'Millan (Aberdeen: George
and Robert King, 1848), 2:422.

2. John Bunyan, *The Pilgrim's Progress*, in *The Works of John Bunyan*, ed. George
Offor (1854; repr., Edinburgh: Banner of Truth, 1991), 3:98.

places thou mayest meet with in the way."[3] It was the portrait of a faithful minister of the Word, called by God to be a trusty guide to a pilgrim people. We can discern in this portrait a summary of the idealized values of the Puritan minister.

The Puritan ideal of the faithful minister is of one who spurns the world, looks to heaven only for his reward, and—not least of all—is a man of the Book. "The best of books [is] in his hand," Bunyan writes. It's also in his conversation: "The law of truth was written upon his lips." Firmly grasping the Word of God, speaking forth the wisdom of God, the Puritan sought to bring all of life under the will of God.

Interpreter tells Christian that this man of the Book is the *only* authorized guide appointed by God. This is not so much because of the man as it is because of the Book that is in his hand. Interpreter warns him: "Take good heed to what I have showed thee, and bear well in thy mind what thou hast seen, lest in thy journey thou meet with some that pretend to lead thee right, but their way goes down to death."[4] There are many deceivers in the world who do not lead by the Book. What distinguishes the true guide from false guides is, above all, the Book. The distinctive characteristic of the sure and safe guide on the way to the Celestial City is that he is driven by Scripture alone.

All of Scripture for All of Life

Sola Scriptura, one of the five "solas," or watchwords of the Protestant Reformation, asserts that Scripture alone is the supreme, infallible authority for Christian faith and life. Known as the "formal principle" of the Protestant Reformation, this watchword summarizes the truth that Scripture is the ultimate criterion for all that we believe and practice. The Puritans inherited a well-developed doctrine of *sola Scriptura* from the Reformers. They

---

3. Bunyan, *The Pilgrim's Progress*, in *Works*, 3:98.
4. Bunyan, *The Pilgrim's Progress*, in *Works*, 3:98.

championed its cause and brought it into fuller practical development as they sought to develop its implications more thoroughly than the Reformers had done in their generation.

We might say that the greatest contribution the Puritans have made to the church's understanding of the Bible is in their uncommon ability to apply its teachings to everyday life. They took profound theological knowledge and turned it into accessible wisdom for living. Taking solid, Reformed, biblical, experiential, confessional Christianity, they applied it to the lives of people in the pew. They excelled in unleashing the full implications of Scripture's doctrine into the context of the nitty gritty affairs of the everyday man. Sharpening Reformed theology into higher definition, they simultaneously sought to apply Scripture to every facet of our existence in God's world.

The result of all this biblical reflection and application was the formation of a Christian worldview. Though the term "worldview" did not come into use until the eighteenth century in Germany, the Puritans certainly had one. They eyed the world around them and looked at themselves through the lenses or spectacles of Holy Scripture. They didn't simply apply the Bible to life; they applied their lives to the Bible, surrendering themselves to the absolute authority of Scripture. They sought to subject God's entire world to God's entire Word. Always concerned with the "use" or practical application of Scripture, they sought to shape every area of life by the Word. Whether marriage, family, politics, work, recreation, stewardship, hobbies, entertainment, friendship, or whatever topic, it was to be formatively mastered by the Word of the Lord.

Peter Lewis wrote in *The Genius of Puritanism* that "Puritanism was not merely a set of rules or a larger creed, but a life-force: a vision and a compulsion which saw the beauty of a holy life and moved towards it, marveling at the possibilities and thrilling to the satisfaction of a God-centred life."[5] This "life-force" combined

---

5. Peter Lewis, *The Genius of Puritanism* (Sussex: Carey Publications Limited, 1979), 12.

a theocentric vision of holy infatuation with God's glory with scrupulous scriptural living. The consequence was that "every area of life came under the influence of God and the guidance of the Word."[6]

In the remainder of this chapter, we consider how the Puritans can help shape our lives by Scripture through the personal reading of the Word and the public preaching of the Word. Then we'll attempt to summarize what they understood about how this influx of biblical truth should be assimilated and applied, namely, in how it should result in a life of consecration and God-oriented piety for the glory of God.

The Reading of the Word

The Puritans believed that the Bible should be the Christian's daily companion. The Scottish, puritan-minded Thomas Boston (1676–1732) said, "The reading of the word is an ordinance of God, and mean[s] of salvation, of God's own appointment. The Bible is this word, and God has given it to us, and appointed it to be read."[7] Boston says that there are three contexts in which God has appointed it to be read.

First, the Bible is to be read in public, in the services of the church (1 Thess. 5:27; 1 Tim. 4:13). In addition to the preaching of the Word of God, the Puritans followed the custom of the early church of *lectio continua*: reading through the Bible book by book, chapter by chapter, in sequence.[8] During these times, there would

---

6. Lewis, *The Genius of Puritanism*, 12.

7. Boston, *An Illustration of the Doctrines of the Christian Religion*, in *Works*, 2:422.

8. Justin Martyr (100–165) describes church worship in the second century: "And on the day called Sunday, all who live in the cities or in the country gather together in one place, and the memoirs of the apostles or the writings of the prophets are read, as long as time permits; then, when the reader has ceased, the president verbally instructs, and exhorts to the imitation of these good things. Then we all rise together and pray" (*First Apology* 1.67; *ANF* 1:186).

be no commenting—just reading the text out loud and listening to it corporately, receiving it and submitting to it, as an act of worship. Second, the Bible is to be read aloud in families. We'll return to that point in a moment. Third, the Bible is to be read in private, the "secret reading of it by one's self." For Boston, to own a Bible and habitually neglect it was a sure sign of a lack of spiritual life. "By this means the soul converses with God in his word. And those who do not make a practice of daily reading the scripture, are none of the Lord's people, whatever otherwise they may profess."[9] If we have tasted of the transforming power of the new birth, we will continually hunger for the pure milk of the Word (1 Peter 2:2). Lack of hunger can only signify sickness, or, tragically, lack of life altogether. "The godly man is a lover of the Word," says Thomas Watson (1620–1686).[10]

As noted above, the Bible must also be read in families. Every family was expected to practice daily family worship in which the head of the family would read and comment on the Scriptures to the rest of the household. Boston said, "Every family ought to be a church; and as they are to speak to God by prayer, so they are to hear God speak to them, by reading his word. And this they ought to do every morning and evening, as well as command their children and servants to read it by themselves."[11] Whether you practice family worship twice daily, as Boston recommends, or once, be sure to read the Word aloud together in the home. "For he established a testimony in Jacob, and appointed a law in Israel, which he commanded our fathers, that they should make them known to their children" (Ps. 78:5).

Why? Because the Bible is a priceless possession! Through the efforts of Christ's servants—men such as William Tyndale (1494–1536) and the Reformers—the Bible became a commonplace

---

9. Boston, *An Illustration of the Doctrines of the Christian Religion*, in *Works*, 2:423.

10. Thomas Watson, *A Godly Man's Picture* (1666; repr., Edinburgh: Banner of Truth, 2009), 60.

11. Boston, *An Illustration of the Doctrines of the Christian Religion*, in *Works*, 2:423.

possession, available to every home. Did Tyndale shed his bold blood to put families in possession of this once forbidden Book only to have it collect dust on the shelf? The Puritans believed that it was to be treasured in the home above any other possession that could possibly adorn the living situation, because it is a Book worth dying for. Plus, there is much profit in making it central to the family's quality time together. The reading of the Bible in families unites family members around the throne of God and joins them together in worship and love, binding their hearts to God and one another.

In Puritan parishes, other literary auxiliaries served to simplify and amplify the teachings of the Bible. When the typical Puritan pastor would assume the call to pastor a congregation, he would normally put in place a system of systematic Christian education. The tool of choice for this task was the trusted catechism, a guide to theology in the form of questions and answers. By using catechisms already in existence or writing their own, Puritan pastors would instruct their congregations on how to make use of them.

The catechism was a doctrinal map that charted out the theological terrain of Scripture. It provided a concise and systematic summary of the major doctrines of the Bible, enabling laypeople to discern these themes in their own reading of Scripture. That way, the Bible could be understood as a unified, coherent whole, the product of God's singular wisdom. John Cotton (1585–1652) titled his catechism *Milk for Babes, Drawn Out of the Breasts of Both Testaments*. Other Puritans included in the titles of their catechisms such expressions as "the main and fundamental points," "the sum of the Christian religion," the "several heads" or "first principles" of religion, and "the ABC of Christianity."[12] By careful pastoral oversight, the Puritans would hold their people accountable for teaching the catechism in their households and for practicing daily family worship.

---

12. Adapted from Joel R. Beeke and Mark Jones, *A Puritan Theology: Doctrine for Life* (Grand Rapids: Reformation Heritage Books, 2012), 963–64.

How many Christians today treasure the public reading of Scripture in church? The Puritans taught their people to cherish it. How many Christians today neglect the daily, private reading of the Scriptures? The Puritans emphasized that we must read our Bibles daily, deliberately, slowly, meditatively, prayerfully, and with experiential application. What about family worship? Does your family gather together around the Bible, or is your family time structured around the television, the computer, and the smartphone, which splinter our gathered families into isolated segments, each in their own little world? Who is discipling our children? Is it Peter and Paul and the pious Reformed giants of the past, or is it Caesar, Hollywood, and the media? The Puritans urge us to have our minds fashioned and renewed by the regular reading of God's Word.

Reading the Scriptures privately and in families is no substitute for corporate worship, however. The church provides the context in which the Spirit ordinarily—and most powerfully—works in conjunction with the Word. Today many Christians think they can be well fed and nourished by private Bible study and sermons on the internet, while they neglect any meaningful participation in the church. That was not the Puritan view. They had a high esteem for the Word in the church.

The Preaching of the Word
"Preach the word" (2 Tim. 4:2), Paul charged Timothy. The Puritans took this charge seriously. The insistence of the Puritans on the primacy of preaching in the church was rooted in their conviction of the divine inspiration, authority, power, and purity of the Word. Being deeply convinced that God builds His church primarily by the instrument of preaching, the Puritans made preaching central to the worship of the church. In this they followed the Reformation as they put the pulpit, rather than the altar, at the center of their churches, and put preaching, rather than the sacraments, at the center of their worship. Richard Sibbes (1577–1635) wrote,

"Preaching is the ordinance of God, sanctified for the begetting of faith, for the opening of the understanding, for the drawing of the will and affections to Christ."[13]

Over five decades ago, Martyn Lloyd-Jones (1899–1981), the gifted expositor known for setting logic on fire in his preaching, and an avid student of the Puritans, lamented:

> We are living in an age which is querying everything, and among these things it is querying the place and the value and the purpose of preaching. In increasing numbers people seem to be depreciating the value of preaching, and they are turning more and more to singing of various types and kinds, accompanied with various kinds of instruments. They are going back also to dramatic representations or recitals of the Scripture, and some are going back even to dancing and various other forms of external manifestations of the act of worship. All this is having the effect of depreciating the place and value of preaching.[14]

The primacy of the Word is being displaced while unauthorized imposters, such as entertainment, usurp Christ's rightful place in the church. This downgrade that is causing the modern church to stray from the Reformation's attention to biblical exposition would have been detested by the Puritans.

Lloyd-Jones says of the Puritans that "to them, preaching was central, and the most important thing of all."[15] Unleashing the written Word through the preached Word served to amplify the meaning of the text, making it come alive and work efficaciously by the Spirit's grace in ways that ordinarily go beyond our private Bible reading. Lloyd-Jones quotes the Puritan Thomas Cartwright

---

13. Richard Sibbes, *The Fountain Opened*, in *The Works of Richard Sibbes* (Edinburgh: Banner of Truth, 2001), 5:514.

14. D. Martyn Lloyd-Jones, *The Puritans: Their Origins and Successors, Addresses Delivered at the Puritan and Westminster Conferences, 1959–1978* (1987; repr., Edinburgh: Banner of Truth, 2014), 373.

15. Lloyd-Jones, *The Puritans*, 375.

(1535–1603), who said, "As the fire stirred giveth more heat, so the Word, as it were, blown by preaching, flameth more in the hearers than when it is read." Commenting on that, Lloyd-Jones said, "The real function of preaching is not to give information, it is to do what Cartwright says; it is to give more heat, to give life to it, to give power to it, to bring it home to the hearers."[16]

Thomas Boston would have agreed: "It is the mercy of the church of God, that they have the word of God as a lamp always burning: but the preaching of it is the snuffing[17] of the lamp, by which it gives the greater light."[18] In another place, Boston wrote,

> The word of God is the sword of the Spirit. We cannot want [lack] it in an evil hour, if we mind to strive against the stream. It is true, the word read is the sword of the Spirit as well as preached. But the preaching of it is the special mean[s] to draw it out of the scabbard, and put it into the hand of poor sinners against their enemies. Thus the Eunuch, after reading the word, replied to Philip's question, "How can I understand it, except some man should guide me?" And he desired that Philip do come up and sit with him for that purpose. The well is deep, and there is need of some to draw for the people, that they may drink.[19]

We too live in an evil hour. The church in our day needs reformation and revival. Biblical illiteracy is becoming the plague of a "post-Christian" culture. We must not sheathe our sword! A high esteem for Scripture will lead to giving a high priority to the public proclamation of it. Those who love God's Word long to broadcast it abroad. We must remember that, as the Reformers taught, "through the words of the preacher, the living voice of the

---

16. Lloyd-Jones, *The Puritans*, 376.
17. That is, the trimming of the lampwick.
18. Boston, *An Illustration of the Doctrines of the Christian Religion*, in *Works*, 2:423.
19. Boston, "Thanksgiving For My Continuance in Ettrick" (Sermon XXVII), in *Works*, 3:373–74.

gospel (*viva vox evangelii*) is heard."[20] Every genuine reformation and revival in history was driven by the anointed unleashing of the Word of God. Where faithful, biblical, Spirit-empowered preaching prospers and is esteemed among the people, spiritual vitality flourishes. God's Word isn't sent forth in vain (Isa. 55:11).

The Word preached, says Thomas Watson, is "a commentary upon the Word written. The Scriptures are the sovereign oils and balsams; the preaching of the Word is the pouring of them out. The Scriptures are the precious spices; the preaching of the Word is the beating of these spices, which causes a wonderful fragrance and delight."[21] He says that the godly person loves the Word when it is preached because by it Christ speaks to us from heaven (Heb. 12:25) and extends His power to save us (1 Cor. 1:24). "The stamp of divine authority on the Word preached makes it an instrument conducive to man's salvation."[22] Sound preaching is like sublime music to the ears of the people of God. "What was once said of the city of Thebes, that it was built by the sound of Amphius' harp, is much more true of soul conversion. It is built by the sound of the gospel harp…. This ministry of the Word is to be preferred before the ministry of angels."[23]

Out of esteem for God, we should treasure the Word in all the forms it comes to us, especially when it is preached. The good we receive from the preached Word refreshes our souls like the dew that fell with the manna. The church needs, in this desperate hour, not just faithful preachers but faithful hearers and receivers of the Word (James 1:21).

---

20. Carl L. Beckwith, Timothy George, and Scott M. Manetsch, eds., *Ezekiel, Daniel: Old Testament*, vol. 12, Reformation Commentary on Scripture (Downers Grove, Ill.: IVP Academic, 2012), xiv.
21. Watson, *A Godly Man's Picture*, 64.
22. Watson, *A Godly Man's Picture*, 65.
23. Watson, *A Godly Man's Picture*, 64.

Extremism or Reasonable Service?

The Puritans were zealous not only to learn the Bible but to live the Bible. Some people think that such zealous attention to the Bible is a bit extreme. A common criticism that has been hurled at the Puritans is the charge of legalism. But their desire to honor the Scriptures in all of life was not driven by any attempt to earn the favor of God or to merit righteousness. They abhorred such a thought and denounced it powerfully in their polemics against all strands of Pelagianism and semi-Pelagianism. Their motivation was not fear of condemnation but gratitude for salvation. They based their experiential application of the imperatives of Scripture on the indicatives of gospel grace.

A good example of this is Romans 12:1: "I beseech you therefore, brethren, by the mercies of God, that ye present your bodies a living sacrifice, holy, acceptable unto God, which is your reasonable service." Jonathan Edwards (1703–1758) exemplifies the Puritan understanding of this text when he says that the exhortation is addressed to those who are "the subjects of God's redeeming mercies."[24] As Edwards points out, the indicative was a reality in them by grace; grounding his exhortation on that, the inspired apostle implores believers to a sanctified life. This is not legalism; it is biblical, gospel-grounded piety. Scripture calls for total consecration as it shapes the whole of life (see 1 Thess. 5:23). In an experiential sermon on Romans 12:1, Edwards asks, "What is offering or giving ourselves up to God?" Listen to what he says (my amplifying comments are interspersed in brackets to show the relevance to the subject before us):

> A willing embracing [of] all God's commands [every precept of His Word], and a devoting ourselves up to God as servants, and receiving him as sovereign, God and King over our souls and bodies, over all our powers and all our actions. 'Tis a

---

24. Jonathan Edwards, *Religious Affections*, in *The Works of Jonathan Edwards,* ed. John E. Smith and Harry S. Stout, revised edition (New Haven: Yale University Press, 2009), 2:343.

giving our understandings to him to be enlightened [by His Word and Spirit], and to be exercised in thinking upon him [especially in meditating on the Word]. 'Tis a giving our wills to him, to be guided and exercised in choosing of him above all things [as our wills are informed by His Word]. 'Tis a giving our affections to him to be governed and exercised in loving him, and what he loves, and hating what he hates [as specified in His Word]. 'Tis a giving all our executive powers to him to be employed wholly in his service [as His will is revealed in His Word].[25]

Though my bracketed comments are not in the original, Edwards would have agreed that they are implied. In his Reformed understanding of the Christian life, such a Word-driven consecration was a given.

God reigns in grace, and He extends that reign to us through Scripture as the Scripture authoritatively shapes every aspect of our lives. Edwards teaches that it should shape our souls and bodies, our powers and actions, our understandings and wills, our affections and all that we are as God's image-bearers. The Word of God must be brought to bear on how we think, how we feel, how we act, how we plan, how we live, and how we love.

This is not extremism; it is our "reasonable service" to our matchless Savior and King! In the words of John Flavel (1628–1691), "If Jesus Christ did wholly set himself apart for believers, *how reasonable is it that believers should consecrate and set themselves apart wholly for Christ?*"[26] Such consecration is driven by the Word. After all, the Lord did pray, "Sanctify them through thy truth; thy word is truth" (John 17:17).

---

25. Jonathan Edwards, "Dedication to God," in *Jonathan Edwards Sermons*, ed. Wilson H. Kimnach (New Haven: Jonathan Edwards Center at Yale University, 1722–1723), Romans 12:1.

26. John Flavel, *The Fountain of Life: A Display of Christ in His Essential and Mediatorial Glory,* in *The Whole Works of the Reverend John Flavel* (London; Edinburgh; Dublin: W. Baynes and Son; Waugh and Innes; M. Keene, 1820), 1:101.

Theocentric, Scripture-Shaped Piety

Because the Puritans had a high view of the Bible, they had a high view of God. Actually, it was their high view of God that led them to have such a high esteem for the Bible, because it is His self-attested, self-authenticating, inspired and precious Word. They "received it not as the word of men, but as it is in truth, the word of God, which effectually worketh also [in them] that believe" (1 Thess. 2:13).

John Flavel comments on the divine authority, commanding power, and transforming efficacy of the Scriptures:

> Can the power of any creature, the word of a mere man, so convince the conscience, so terrify the heart, so discover the very secret thoughts of the soul, as to put a man into such tremblings? No, a greater than man must needs be here; none but a God can so open the eyes of the blind, so open the graves of the dead, so quicken and enliven the conscience that was seared, so bind over the soul of a sinner to the judgment to come, so change and alter the frame and temper of a man's spirit, or so powerfully raise, refresh and comfort a drooping dying soul; certainly the power of God is in all this; and, if there were no more, yet this alone were sufficient to make full proof of the divine authority of the scriptures.[27]

Flavel draws attention to a common theme in Puritan writings. In their respect for the Bible, the Puritans made much of Isaiah 66:2: "To this man will I look, even to him that is poor and of a contrite spirit, and trembleth at my word." They understood this trembling to be that of a filial fear toward God as Holy Father, a sincere reverence that led them to hang upon every detail of the Word with a humble heart and attentive conscience. The Puritan conscience was captive to God by the Word.

J. I. Packer said, "The concern which was really supreme in the minds and hearts of the people called Puritans was a concern

---

27. Flavel, *The Method of Grace in the Gospel Redemption,* in *Works,* 2:300.

about God—a concern to know him truly, and serve him rightly, and so to glorify him and to enjoy him."[28] In serving God, Packer tells us, the Puritans placed great emphasis on the necessity of securing and maintaining a clean conscience—one that, having been cleansed by Christ's blood, is informed by the Bible. Packer explains how the soul of Puritan spirituality pertained to the inner life of the conscience, which "signified a man's knowledge of himself as standing in God's presence (*coram Deo*, in Luther's phrase), subject to God's word and exposed to the judgement of God's law, and yet—if a believer—justified and accepted nonetheless through divine grace."[29] Living for God's glory meant serving Him out of a justified and purified conscience, and serving Him with a clean conscience meant bringing the enlightened conscience into full and integral subjection to the Book by the grace of the gospel.

The Christian life must be Bible-driven because the Christian heart is to be Bible-governed. Packer writes, "To them, there could be no real spiritual understanding, nor any genuine godliness, except as men exposed and enslaved their consciences to God's word."[30] True piety, according to the Puritans, is the living Word of God exercising its efficacious influence on the totality of our human existence, from the inner life of the heart to the outward life of practical living. Puritan devotion sought to engage the whole person with the whole Scripture, bringing every faculty of the human constitution into conformity to the whole counsel of God. That is what it means to bring *sola Scriptura* into holistic application—to be zealously consumed with a theocentric worldview that seeks to bring all of creation under the authoritative Scriptures to the praise of God.

28. J. I. Packer, *A Quest for Godliness: The Puritan Vision of the Christian Life* (Wheaton, Ill.: Crossway, 1990), 107.
29. Packer, *A Quest for Godliness*, 108.
30. Packer, *A Quest for Godliness*, 107.

Contagious Love for the Scriptures

The Puritans shape our minds according to the Bible. They loved the Bible, lived the Bible, sang the Bible, preached the Bible, read the Bible, memorized the Bible. They were thinking about the Bible every day. They were Bible-shaped theologians and Bible-shaped preachers. They just thought that way—that's who they were. We need more of that focus on the Word of God today.

If you read the Puritans regularly, their focus on the Scriptures becomes contagious. Though their commentaries on Scripture are not the last word in exegesis, they show how to yield wholehearted allegiance to the Bible's message. The Puritans themselves would not have us to hold them in high esteem but would point us to Christ, who comes to us through the means of grace, the chief of which is Scripture. By their faithful teaching, they bring the Bible to us more practically; their sincere goal was that they could bring us to the Bible more devotedly, more fully, more holistically.

What better way to pore over the Scriptures than to have these seasoned pastor-theologians standing over our shoulders as we read, and by their writings suggesting to us the best of their insights as we meditate on the meaning of the matchless words of God! If we invite them to be our companions as we study God's Book, we may veritably come to experience in greater measure the truth of the Scripture that says, "He that walketh with wise men shall be wise" (Prov. 13:20). That is our prayer as you read these pages—not that you would be driven merely to the Puritans but that through the testimony of the Puritans you may be driven further into the Scriptures, and further into communion with the triune God of grace and glory.

Questions for Reflection and Discussion

1. Why is devotion to Scripture and a concern with obedience to its commands not legalism? Meditate on Romans 12:1 and the relationship between the mercies of God and our grateful response of consecration, obedience, and worship.

2. What do your personal and family practices of Bible reading and meditation reflect about the importance and centrality of Scripture to your Christian life? Has something else displaced Scripture in your life?

3. Do you view regularly hearing the preached Word in corporate worship as a means of grace? If God truly speaks to us through the preached Word, how ought this to shape our thoughts and change our practices?

THE PURITANS
Lift Our Gaze to the Greatness
and Glory of the Triune God

The highest science, the loftiest speculation, the mightiest philosophy, which can ever engage the attention of a child of God, is the name, the nature, the person, the work, the doings, and the existence of the great God whom he calls his Father.
—CHARLES H. SPURGEON[1]

The story is told of a little boy who was absorbed in drawing a picture as his admiring father watched. The father was curious. His son was so focused, so riveted in crafting his creative masterpiece. What could it be? "What are you drawing, son?" he asked. Without even looking up, the boy answered, "God." Rather surprised, the father decided it was time to gently shape his son's theology. "Well, no one knows what God looks like," he said. Without missing a beat, his son replied, "They will when I'm finished!"

How typical of our innate tendency to reduce God to the limits of our own imaginations! As someone once said, "God made man in his own image, and man returned the compliment." God Himself, speaking through the psalmist, agreed: "Thou thoughtest that I was altogether such an one as thyself" (Ps. 50:21). The

---

1. Charles H. Spurgeon, "The Immutability of God," in *The New Park Street Pulpit* (London: Passmore & Alabaster, 1855; repr. Pasadena, Tex.: Pilgrim Publications, 1975), 1:1.

temptation to create a god in our own image is still with us. As the Reformer John Calvin (1509–1564) said, "Man's nature, so to speak, is a perpetual factory of idols."[2] We desperately need faithful guides to instruct us in the true knowledge of God.

The famous nineteenth-century Baptist pastor Charles Spurgeon (1834–1892) loved the Puritans and quoted them often. In his first published sermon in the New Park Street Pulpit, he said, "The highest science, the loftiest speculation, the mightiest philosophy, which can ever engage the attention of a child of God, is the name, the nature, the person, the work, the doings, and the existence of the great God whom he calls his Father."[3] To this the Puritans would have declared a resounding "Amen!" They were convinced that our life, salvation, comfort, holiness, and joy are built on the solid foundation of a saving knowledge of God in Christ through the Spirit. In the words of George Swinnock (1627–1673), "Our eternal happiness consists in large part in our perfect knowledge of the blessed and boundless God."[4] In their sermons and treatises, the Puritans lift our gaze upward to our triune God in His transcendent, soul-satisfying greatness and glory. They encourage and exhort us to know God according to His self-revelation, to know God experientially, and to know God in Christ.

Knowing God According to His Self-Revelation

The Puritans rightly believed that though "the magnitude of God's perfections is well beyond the reach of our finite understanding," yet "we can know what He has chosen to reveal."[5]

---

2. John Calvin, *Institutes of the Christian Religion*, ed. John T. McNeill, trans. Ford Lewis Battles, The Library of Christian Classics (Louisville, Ky.: Westminster John Knox Press, 2011), 1.11.8.

3. Spurgeon, "The Immutability of God," in *The New Park Street Pulpit*, 1:1.

4. George Swinnock, *The Blessed and Boundless God* (Grand Rapids: Reformation Heritage Books, 2014), 1.

5. Swinnock, *The Blessed and Boundless God,* 2.

On the one hand, God is incomparable and incomprehensible. "For who in the heaven can be compared unto the LORD? who among the sons of the mighty can be likened unto the LORD?" (Ps. 89:6). But on the other hand, God has made Himself known by revealing Himself through His works (Ps. 8:1; 19:1–6; Rom. 1:18–20); His Word (Ps. 19:7–11; Heb. 1:1); and supremely in His incarnate Son, the Lord Jesus Christ (John 17:3; Heb. 1:2; 1 John 5:20).

As we saw in the previous chapter, this conviction grounded the Puritans' sermons, discourses, and theological treatises in the clear teaching of Scripture, making them reliable, helpful guides for believers today. What Spurgeon once said of John Bunyan could be said of all the best Puritan divines: "Read anything of his, and you will see that it is almost like reading the Bible itself. He had read it till his very soul was saturated with Scripture…. Prick him anywhere—his blood is Bibline, the very essence of the Bible flows from him. He cannot speak without quoting a text, for his very soul is full of the Word of God."[6] The writings of the Puritans are saturated with Scripture. They were profoundly biblical thinkers, gripped with a passion for knowing, loving, and obeying God.

One of the finest examples is Swinnock's *The Incomparableness of God,* recently reprinted in a modernized edition as *The Blessed and Boundless God.*[7] Swinnock's book-length meditation on Psalm 89:6 (quoted above) is a careful and practical study of God's being, attributes, works, and words.

Swinnock wrote about the incomparable excellence of God's being, showing that God's being is independent, perfect, universal, unchangeable, eternal, simple, infinite, and incomprehensible.[8]

---

6. *C. H. Spurgeon's Autobiography Compiled from His Diary, Letters, and Records, Vol. IV: 1878–1892* (London: Passmore & Alabaster, 1900; repr. Pasadena, Tex.: Pilgrim Publications, 1992), 268.

7. George Swinnock, *The Incomparableness of God*, in *The Works of George Swinnock* (Edinburgh: James Nichol, 1868; repr. Edinburgh: Banner of Truth, 1996), vol. 4.

8. Swinnock, *The Blessed and Boundless God,* part 1.

He began by asserting that "God is His own first cause" and "His own last end."[9] Angelic and human beings derive their existence from God, but God is entirely self-existent, dependent on no one. Furthermore, "God is altogether for Himself as His highest end. He is His own end as well as His own beginning. He never had a 'beginning' nor will He ever have an 'ending' (Rev. 1:8). He does what He does for Himself."[10] Swinnock established, from Scripture, the truth that "the chief end of God is to glorify God and enjoy Himself forever."[11]

In the course of his book, Swinnock considered at least sixteen specific attributes of God. He defined God's attributes as "those perfections in the divine nature which are ascribed to Him so that we can better understand Him. They are called *attributes* because they are attributed to Him for our sake, even though they are not in Him as they are in humans or angels."[12]

Swinnock's definitions of these attributes are rooted in Scripture, clearly explained, and simply expressed. For example:

- God's *power* is that attribute by which He effects whatever He pleases.[13]

- God's *justice* is that attribute whereby He disposes all things according to the rule of equity and renders to all people according to their works.[14]

- *Knowledge* is that attribute of God whereby He understands all things in and of Himself.[15]

---

9. Swinnock, *The Blessed and Boundless God,* 11.
10. Swinnock, *The Blessed and Boundless God,* 12.
11. John Piper, *Desiring God: Meditations of a Christian Hedonist* (Sisters, Ore.: Multnomah Publishers, 2003), 31. Piper is, of course, adapting from the Westminster Shorter Catechism's first question: "What is the chief end of man?"
12. Swinnock, *The Blessed and Boundless God,* 35.
13. Swinnock, *The Blessed and Boundless God,* 44.
14. Swinnock, *The Blessed and Boundless God,* 47.
15. Swinnock, *The Blessed and Boundless God,* 50.

• *Mercy* is an attribute of God whereby He pities us in our misery.[16]

• *Patience* is that attribute of God whereby He bears with sinners, deferring their punishment or awaiting their conversion.[17]

Throughout the book, Swinnock focuses the gaze of his readers on the incomparable greatness of God, who "is boundless in His duration, perfections, attributes, and being."[18] In addition to God's being and attributes, Swinnock also covered God's incomparable works (including His works of creation, providence, and redemption) and words.[19]

Swinnock is just one example among the many Puritan writers who taught believers to meditate on God's greatness and glory. In his sermons on the Westminster Shorter Catechism, Thomas Watson explained and applied the fourth question and answer by considering the being, knowledge, eternity, unchangeableness, wisdom, power, holiness, justice, mercy, truth, and unity of God, along with the doctrines of the Trinity, creation, and providence.[20] Stephen Charnock (1628–1680) wrote a magisterial treatment of God's existence and attributes,[21] which is "perhaps the most extensive and incisive Puritan treatise on the doctrine of God."[22] This theological and devotional feast could provide months (if not

---

16. Swinnock, *The Blessed and Boundless God,* 57.

17. Swinnock, *The Blessed and Boundless God,* 60.

18. Swinnock, *The Blessed and Boundless God,* 27.

19. Swinnock, *The Blessed and Boundless God,* parts 3 and 4, respectively.

20. Thomas Watson, *A Body of Divinity: Contained in Sermons Upon the Westminster Assembly's Catechism* (1692; repr. Edinburgh: Banner of Truth, 2003), 39–127. The catechism reads, "Q. What is God? A. God is a spirit, infinite, eternal, and unchangeable in his being, wisdom, power, holiness, justice, goodness, and truth."

21. Stephen Charnock, *The Existence and Attributes of God* (New York: Robert Carter & Brothers, 1853; repr., Grand Rapids: Baker, 1996). This work is also found in volumes 1 and 2 of *The Complete Works of Stephen Charnock, B. D.* (Edinburgh: James Nichol, 1865; repr., Edinburgh: Banner of Truth, 2010).

22. Joel R. Beeke and Mark Jones, *A Puritan Theology: Doctrine for Life* (Grand Rapids: Reformation Heritage Books, 2012), 59.

years!) of nourishment to believers hungry to know God. For a taste, consider this reflection on the beauty of God's holiness:

> As his power is the strength of [his perfections], so his holiness is the beauty of them. As all would be weak, without almightiness to back them, so all would be uncomely without holiness to adorn them…. Holiness is the rule of all his acts, the source of all his punishments. If every attribute of the Deity were a distinct member, purity would be the form, the soul, the spirit to animate them. Without it, his patience would be an indulgence to sin, his mercy a fondness, his wrath a madness, his power a tyranny, his wisdom an unworthy subtlety. It is this [that] gives a decorum to all.[23]

Knowing God in Christ

The Puritans also insisted that we can never truly know God apart from His Son, Jesus Christ. Jesus Himself said, "And this is life eternal, that they might know thee the only true God, and Jesus Christ, whom thou hast sent" (John 17:3). In his discourse on this text, Charnock derived two doctrines:

> Doctrine I. The knowledge of God and Christ the Mediator is the necessary means to eternal life and happiness.

> Doctrine II. The true and saving knowledge of God is only in and by Christ.[24]

This underscores an important and characteristic emphasis of the Puritans: they were evangelical (that is, focused on the gospel) and Christ-centered in their pastoral theology and practice.

Owen placed such a high premium on this that he listed it as the first of four evidences of saving faith. "The most basic act

---

23. Charnock, *Existence and Attributes of God,* 2:113–14.

24. Stephen Charnock, "A Discourse of the Knowledge of God," in *The Complete Works of Stephen Charnock, B. D.* (Edinburgh: James Nichol, 1865; repr., Edinburgh: Banner of Truth, 2010), 4:110. Charnock's two discourses on the knowledge of God are distinct from the longer book on God's existence and attributes referenced earlier.

of saving faith," he said, "is choosing, embracing, and approving of God's way of saving sinners by the mediation of Jesus Christ, relying on Him alone, while renouncing all other alleged ways and means of salvation."[25]

In a day in which religious pluralism constantly threatens to blunt the sharp edges in our profession of the Christian faith, the Puritans' focus on Christ as the exclusive Mediator between God and man is essential. This is important for at least three reasons.

1. God is supremely glorified through Christ's work as our Mediator. This is evident in Jesus's prayer just prior to his betrayal and crucifixion: "Father, the hour is come; glorify thy Son, that thy Son also may glorify thee: As thou hast given him power over all flesh, that he should give eternal life to as many as thou hast given him" (John 17:1–2).

"The hour" in John's gospel often refers to the hour of Christ's crucifixion (see John 2:4; 7:30; 8:20; 12:23, 27; 13:1). But the hour of His crucifixion is also the hour of His exaltation and glorification with the Father. Why? Because through the cross God displayed the glory of His manifold perfections. "Only that which corresponds to God's infinite wisdom, goodness, grace, holiness, and righteousness is worthy of God," writes Owen. "And this is what faith discerns and approves concerning the way of salvation: that it is worthy of God in every way. It answers every aspect of His holy being."[26]

This is beautifully expressed in the words of a wonderful hymn by William Rees (1802–1883):

> On the mount of crucifixion
> Fountains opened deep and wide;

---

25. John Owen, *Gospel Evidences of Saving Faith* (Grand Rapids: Reformation Heritage Books, 2016), 3. This is a modernized version of a treatise titled *Gospel Grounds and Evidences of the Faith of God's Elect*, in *The Works of John Owen*, ed. W. H. Goold (1850–1853; repr., Edinburgh: Banner of Truth, 1966), 5:401–57.

26. Owen, *Gospel Evidences of Saving Faith*, 14.

Through the floodgates of God's mercy
Flowed a vast and gracious tide.
Grace and love, like mighty rivers,
Poured incessant from above,
And heav'n's peace and perfect justice
Kissed a guilty world in love.[27]

2. God is known as our gracious Father through Christ. God's revelation in creation is sufficient to show His power and glory, thus rendering us without excuse for our rebellion and sin (Rom. 1:19–20). But the good news of God's justifying grace comes only through the revelation of God's redemptive work in Christ (Rom. 3:21–26; 2 Tim. 1:9–10).

Do you remember Jesus's words to His disciples in John 14? "I am the way, the truth, and the life: no man cometh unto the Father, but by me. If ye had known me, ye should have known my Father also: and from henceforth ye know him, and have seen him" (John 14:6–7).

To this Philip replies, "Lord, show us the Father, and it sufficeth us. Jesus saith unto him, Have I been so long time with you, and yet hast thou not known me, Philip? he that hath seen me hath seen the Father" (vv. 8–9). Jesus reveals the heart and character of the Father. Apart from Christ, God can be known only as Creator, Sovereign, Lawgiver, and Judge. But through Christ, we grasp God as our Father. Charnock well captures the importance of knowing God in Christ:

> We must know God to know our duty; we must know Christ
> to know the way of performing it; we must know God,
> therefore, in the perfections of his nature, and Christ in the
> sufficiency of his mediation. We must know God in his rav-
> ishing goodness, his affrighting justice, his condescending
> mercy, his adorable wisdom, his unshaken veracity; we must

---

27. William Rees, "Here is Love Vast as the Ocean," a nineteenth-century hymn known as "the love song of the Welsh Revival."

know him as offended by sin, as pacified by Christ. Without the one, we shall not be humbled; without the other, we shall not approach to him. We must know him in his precepts, else how can we obey him? In his promises, else how can we trust him? We must know Christ in his offices, as an atoning priest, as an instructing prophet, a protecting and governing king. We must know him in his transaction with his Father, descent to the world, we must know him upon the cross and upon the throne, and the ends of both his states: Phil. 3:10, 'Know him, and the power of his resurrection, and the fellowship of his sufferings.' How else can we be 'conformed to his death,' or have confidence in his life?… Without this knowledge, how can we believe in him? How can we love him? How can we perform those acts which are necessary to our salvation?[28]

3. God's promises are given and fulfilled in Christ. The third reason we must know God in Christ is that all of God's promises are given and fulfilled in Christ: "For all the promises of God in him are yea, and in him Amen, unto the glory of God by us" (2 Cor. 1:20).

As the covenant head of God's chosen people, Christ is the single Representative who wins our salvation through His doing and dying. His atoning death cancels our debt. His perfect righteousness covers our nakedness. His resurrection assures us that death does not have the final word. And as our exalted and triumphant king, He now shares the spoils of war with His people. As Paul says, God the Father has "raised him from the dead, and set him at his own right hand in the heavenly places, far above all principality, and power, and might, and dominion, and every name that is named, not only in this world, but also in that which is to come: and hath put all things under his feet, and gave him to be the head over all things to the church, which is his body, the fulness of him that filleth all in all" (Eph. 1:20–23). But our only access to this fullness is through union with Christ Himself.

---

28. Charnock, "A Discourse of the Knowledge of God," in *Works,* 4:25.

Knowing God Experientially

When I was a teenager, I worked for a local printer. Since one of my regular tasks was cleaning the presses, I often ended the workday with ink-covered hands. I soon discovered a wonderful product called Boraxo, a heavy-duty, powdered soap that cleansed my hands down to the very pores of my skin. Boraxo was far more effective than ordinary hand soap. Granted, my hands were usually a bit red and raw when I finished washing—but they were clean!

To read the Puritans is to apply the deep-cleansing properties of truth to our sin-soiled hearts and hands. This is, at least in part, what they meant by "experiential" or "experimental" preaching and theology.[29]

The Puritans were not only theologians but were also pastors. As such, they wanted people to experience deep transformation in their lives rather than rest in a speculative or theoretical knowledge of God. In fact, the Puritans would have said that any theology that was not pastoral fell short of true theology.

John Owen, for example, argued that the ends of true theology were "the cultivation of a most holy and sweet communion with God, wherein lies the true happiness of mankind" and "the celebration of the praise of God, and His glory and grace in the eternal salvation of sinners."[30] To truly know God is to increase in

---

29. For the historical background of this terminology and the etymological roots of the words "experiential" and "experimental," see Joel R. Beeke, *Reformed Preaching: Proclaiming God's Word from the Heart of the Preacher to the Heart of His People* (Wheaton, Ill.: Crossway, 2018), 24–36. "The word *experimental* comes from a Latin root meaning 'to try, prove, or test.' Calvin did not wonder whether Christianity would crash like an experimental airplane. The 'experiment' envisaged is not testing the Bible, but testing *us* by the Bible. The root for *experimental* also shows up in the word *experiential*. Experimental preaching stresses the need to know the great truths of the Word of God by personal experience. It also tests our experience by the doctrines of the Bible. It brings truth to the heart to illuminate who we are, where we stand with God, how we need to be healed, and where we need to be headed" (*Reformed Preaching*, 24–25).

30. John Owen, *Biblical Theology*, trans. Stephen P. Westcott (Morgan, Pa.: Soli Deo Gloria, 1994), 618–19.

holiness, experience a growing communion with God as Father, Son, and Spirit, and devote ourselves to a life of worship for His praise, honor, and glory.

This is why the Puritans were never content with a merely theoretical understanding of God. Watson and Charnock both applied the doctrines they expounded with multiple "uses," while part 5 of Swinnock's *Blessed and Boundless God* is entirely focused on application, arguing that the knowledge of God "affects the heart with love for Him, fear of Him, and hatred for whatever is contrary to Him. True knowledge takes the heart as well as the head."[31]

Experiential theology, then, involves the marriage of mind and heart. It requires both filling our thoughts and firing our affections with divine truth, so that biblical doctrine forms and shapes our personal lives. In the words of Stephen Charnock,

> This knowledge of God is not only a knowledge of God and Christ in theory, but such a knowledge which is saving, joined with ardent love to him; cordial trust in him…. It must therefore be such a knowledge which descends from the head to the heart, which is light in the mind and heat in the affections; such a knowledge of God as includes faith in him.[32]

It is this pastoral concern that accounts for the frequent Puritan practice of dividing their discourses and sermons into (1) the "opening" or exposition of a text; (2) its "doctrine," that is, its theological proposition; and (3) its "use" or application.[33] To put it simply, the Puritans did not want their readers to merely know *about* God. They wanted them *to know God*.

Charnock expounded seven effects of a true knowledge of God. First, he said it is a *transforming* knowledge. Those who behold "the glory of God in the face of Christ" (2 Cor. 4:6) are transformed into the same image from one degree of glory to another, by the

31. Swinnock, *The Blessed and Boundless God,* 140.

32. Charnock, "A Discourse of the Knowledge of God," in *Works,* 4:10.

33. For further explanation, see Sinclair B. Ferguson, "Puritans: Ministers of the Word" in *Some Pastors and Teachers* (Edinburgh: Banner of Truth, 2017), 167–92.

powerful work of God's Spirit (3:18). Where there is no transformation, there is no grace. "That knowledge of God which is not beautified with grace," said Charnock, "instead of making us amiable Christians, will render us deformed devils."[34]

Second, it is an *affective* knowledge, that is, knowledge accompanied by spiritual affections. "What shines upon the head kindles love in the heart.... Both must go together: knowledge without affections is stupid, and affections without knowledge are childish.... If knowledge in the head doth not work spiritual affections in the heart, it can never be put upon the account of a saving knowledge; it is not really knowledge, but only a pretense to it."[35]

Third, a true knowledge of God is *active* and *expressive*. "It expresseth in the life what is in the head and heart."[36] As we read in the letter from James, faith without works is dead (James 2:17, 20, 26).

Fourth, it is *humbling*. A true knowledge of God will always lead to a humble assessment of ourselves. Do you remember what Isaiah said after seeing God's glorious holiness in the temple? "Then said I, Woe is me! for I am undone; because I am a man of unclean lips, and I dwell in the midst of a people of unclean lips: for mine eyes have seen the King, the LORD of hosts" (Isa. 6:5).

The fifth characteristic effect of knowing God is that it takes away our appetite for sin and the world. In Charnock's words, "It is a *weaning* knowledge."[37] Oh, how we need this today! Do you struggle with an "addiction" to television or social media? Are you infected with the disease of "affluenza"? The only way to combat worldliness is by a deeper friendship with God.

Sixth, it is a "knowledge *of faith*."[38] It is knowledge characterized by trust in God. As the psalmist said, "they that know thy name will put their trust in thee" (Ps. 9:10).

---

34. Charnock, "A Discourse of the Knowledge of God," in *Works*, 4:44.
35. Charnock, "A Discourse of the Knowledge of God," in *Works*, 4:45, 47.
36. Charnock, "A Discourse of the Knowledge of God," in *Works*, 4:49.
37. Charnock, "A Discourse of the Knowledge of God," in *Works*, 4:56.
38. Charnock, "A Discourse of the Knowledge of God," in *Works*, 4:57.

Finally, a true, saving knowledge of God is "a *progressive* knowledge, still aiming at more knowledge, and more improvements of it."[39] That is why Paul prayed that the Colossians would increase in the knowledge of God (Col. 1:10) and Peter exhorted believers to "grow in grace, and in the knowledge of our Lord and Saviour Jesus Christ" (2 Peter 3:18).

Years ago, I came across the story of an old gentleman and his son who shared a mutual love for art. The father was a wealthy man with money to spend and, together with his son, enjoyed traveling around the world to purchase rare portraits and paintings for their growing collection. But then the man's son went away to fight in the war. Day after day, the father waited for news of his son, hoping for the day when they would be reunited. But sadly, the old man one day received a telegram informing him that his son had been killed in battle.

Though the father grieved the loss of his son, he found some measure of comfort when a package was delivered the following Christmas. When he unwrapped it, he discovered a portrait of his son. It became, of course, the most treasured piece in his entire art collection.

The old man eventually passed away, leaving his art collection behind to be sold in an auction. Art collectors from around the world came with great interest in his famous collection. When the auction began, the first painting up for sale was the portrait of his son. The auctioneer tried to sell it for a modest price but received no bids. Finally, one of the gentleman's former neighbors placed a small bid and won the piece. The gavel fell. Sold.

The art collectors then waited with hushed breath for the auction to resume. Who would win the rare masterpieces in this famous collection? But to their shock and dismay, the auctioneer announced, "The auction is over. The proceedings are finished." Stunned disbelief filled the room. "What do you mean, 'it's over?'"

---

39. Charnock, "A Discourse of the Knowledge of God," in *Works,* 4:60.

someone asked. "It's very simple," said the auctioneer. "According to the will, whoever gets the son, gets all."

Though I didn't find this story in the Puritan archives, I think they would have approved, for it aptly illustrates the testimony of Scripture, "that God hath given to us eternal life, and this life is in his Son. He that hath the Son hath life; and he that hath not the Son of God hath not life" (1 John 5:11–12).

Dear friend, allow me to ask you: *Do you know God?* I'm not asking merely whether you know about God. But do you know Him as He is revealed in Scripture, in a personal, experiential, life-transforming way? Do you know Him, through Christ, as your gracious Father? If you do truly know Him, are you growing in your acquaintance with Him? Are you increasing in the grace and knowledge of our Lord Jesus Christ? The Puritans can help you in your quest to know God more deeply.

As we conclude this chapter, consider these words from the conclusion of Charnock's sermon:

> Let us behold his justice, to humble ourselves under it; his pardoning grace, to have recourse to it under pressures of guilt. Let us sweeten our affections by the sight of his compassions, and have confidence to call upon him as a Father in our necessities. Not any discovery of God in Christ, but is an encouragement to a forlorn creature, lost in his own sense. His perfections smile upon man; nothing of God looks terrible in Christ to a believer. The sun is risen, shadows are vanished, God walks upon the battlements of love, justice hath left its sting in a Saviour's side, the law is disarmed, weapons out of his hand, his bosom open, his bowels yearn, his heart pants, sweetness and love is in all his carriage. And this is life eternal, to know God believingly in the glories of his mercy and justice in Jesus Christ.[40]

---

40. Charnock, "A Discourse of the Knowledge of God," in *Works,* 4:163.

Questions for Reflection and Discussion

1. If someone were to ask you to describe God, how would you answer? Would you quote from the Scriptures and point them to Jesus? Are your conceptions of God's character rooted in God's revelation of Himself in His written Word and in the Word made flesh?

2. Why can we only know God through Jesus Christ? If Christ was not your mediator, how would that affect your relationship with God?

3. Charnock described several aspects of a saving knowledge of God: it is transforming, affective, active, and humbling; it weans us from the world, is the knowledge of faith, and is progressive. Does this describe your experience of knowing God?

THE PURITANS
Convict Our Consciences of the Subtlety and Sinfulness of Sin

---

As in God there is no evil, so in sin there is no good. God is the chiefest of goods and sin is the chiefest of evils. As no good can be compared with God for goodness, so no evil can be compared with sin for evil.
—RALPH VENNING[1]

When Paul was on trial before Felix, he said in his defense, "Herein do I exercise myself, to have always a conscience void of offence toward God, and toward men" (Acts 24:16). Likewise, to the Corinthians he said, "Our rejoicing is this, the testimony of our conscience, that in simplicity and godly sincerity, not with fleshly wisdom, but by the grace of God, we have had our conversation in the world" (2 Cor. 1:12). The life of piety is one that seeks to procure a conscience free from rendering an internal verdict of "guilty"; as Paul described in another place, "holding the mystery of the faith with a pure conscience" (1 Tim. 3:9). Scripture places much emphasis on the necessity of maintaining a clean conscience.

But what do we do when sin registers its guilt in our conscience? This will inevitably happen, since sin still dwells in the best of saints. Paul confessed in Romans 7:18, "I know that in me

---

1. Ralph Venning, *The Sinfulness of Sin* (1671; repr., Edinburgh: Banner of Truth, 2008), 31.

(that is, in my flesh,) dwelleth no good thing." He complained of a "law of sin," or an operative principle of sin's effectual influence and power, that warred with his inner man (Rom. 7:23). John said, "If we say that we have no sin, we deceive ourselves, and the truth is not in us" (1 John 1:8). These seasoned apostles, advanced in the life of faith, confessed that they yet battled with indwelling sin, just like the rest of us.

This means there is a paradox that rings true in the life of every Christian. On one hand, a pure conscience must be prized and maintained. On the other hand, sin exerts its operative influence and registers itself continually in the consciousness—and conscience—of the Christian. How can we maintain a clear conscience if sin still remains in our consciousness? There is a *wrong* way to cope with this tension and a *right* way to deal with it—which is the way the Puritans taught.

The wrong way would be to try to ignore the consciousness of our sin. Just brush it off. Fall into sin, or allow indwelling sin to register its guilt in your conscience, and then say, "It's no big deal. Everybody does it." Then continue on your merry way. Do all that is in your power to squelch any conviction of guilt. The Puritans would say that such an attitude is pure presumption of personal salvation, but will only pave the way to hell for you. John Bunyan warned, "Take heed of giving thyself liberty of committing one sin, for that will lead thee to another; till, by an ill custom, it become natural. To begin a sin, is to lay a foundation for a continuance; this continuance is the mother of custom, and impudence at last the issue."[2]

Maintaining a pure conscience does not mean that our consciences should become desensitized to sin. Most people attempt to silence the cries of their guilty consciences by suppressing the truth in unrighteousness. As fallen creatures, sin blinds our minds and stupefies our discernment. We tend to downplay the gravity

---

2. John Bunyan, *Bunyan's Dying Sayings*, in *The Works of John Bunyan*, ed. George Offor (1854; repr., Edinburgh: Banner of Truth, 1991), 1:65.

of sin. We seek to cope with our guilt by minimizing our sin. Even many preachers today, when they preach convicting truths, often lighten the atmosphere by telling jokes or making apologies in order to alleviate the weight of conviction. These are wrong ways to try to cope with sin.

The Puritans, like the prophets of old, emphasized the gravity of sin. They labored to expose it in its monstrosity, its heinousness, its power—to highlight its exceeding sinfulness. They probed the conscience with the instrument of the law in order to pierce the disease of sin with truth, to discern and expose it for what it is. They also made much of the grace of the gospel as the only, all-sufficient remedy for sin. The Puritans desired that their hearers and readers would all come to experience a genuine work of grace and have hearts full of assurance. But they insisted that the disease needs to be exposed for the remedy to be appreciated. They also taught that this exposure and appreciation are not limited to a one-time experience leading up to conversion but correspond to an ongoing awareness and growth in the Christian life.

In this chapter, I want to summarize how the Puritans convict our consciences of the sinfulness of sin. We will consider sin in relation to God, in relation to man, and in relation to the Christian. Then we will seek to answer the initial question we posed: how we may face the consciousness of sin while securing and maintaining a clean conscience. We'll conclude with some Puritan wisdom on how to handle this paradoxical tension in a God-honoring way.

Sin in Relation to God

In 1665–1666, the Great Plague struck London with the horrific blow of the bubonic plague. The epidemic is believed to have been caused through the bite of infected rat fleas. In less than two years, the plague killed about 100,000 people—about a quarter of the entire population of London. The Puritan Ralph Venning (1621–1674) had written a treatise and was nearly done with it when the plague struck, but it was not published until four years later. In remembrance of the epidemic, he named his treatise *The Plague of Plagues*.[3] It dealt, however, not with the Great Plague of London but with the great plague of the human heart, one that has infected all of Adam's posterity and is always fatal.

The Great Plague was horrendous, but the plague of sin is infinitely worse. Venning begins his treatment of the subject by situating the reality of sin within a theocentric context. He points out that, in Romans 7:13, the reason sin is shown to be "exceeding sinful" is that the law exposes it as such. Venning says that the sinfulness of sin consists in the fact that it is "the transgression of God's law"[4] (1 John 3:4). He conceptualizes sin in reference to its Godward orientation. That is the first and foremost reason sin is grave: because of "sin's contrariety to God."[5]

Today sin is often lamented over only because of its consequences. Since it destroys marriages, ruins lives, and wreaks havoc on God's good order, people grieve over the temporal consequences of sin and what it does in our fallen world. But few "sigh and…cry" (Ezek. 9:4) over the abomination of sin because it is such a great offense against God. David cried, "Against thee, thee only, have I sinned" (Ps. 51:4). Jonathan Edwards observed, "'Tis fit that God should have the punishment of sin in his own hands, because sin is committed against him, and him only. Others may indeed be injured by it, but sin is against none as it is against God."[6] When you become aware of your sin, what grieves you more? That it causes harm to you or others, or that it offends and grieves the heart of God?[7]

---

3. "Publisher's Introduction" in Venning, *The Sinfulness of Sin*, 15.

4. Venning, *The Sinfulness of Sin*, 29.

5. Venning, *The Sinfulness of Sin*, 29.

6. Jonathan Edwards, "Vengeance for Sin," in *Jonathan Edwards Sermons*, ed. Wilson H. Kimnach (New Haven, Conn.: Jonathan Edwards Center at Yale University, 1730), Deut. 32:35.

7. It should be clarified that when the Puritans speak of grieving God, they are speaking anthropomorphically. But this does not in any way lesson the reality. Thomas Watson, commenting on how sin grieves the Holy Spirit according

Venning teaches that sin is contrary to God in many ways. He says that "sin is contrary to the nature of God."[8] God in His holiness is utterly opposed to sin. "As in God there is no evil, so in sin there is no good. God is the chiefest of goods and sin is the chiefest of evils. As no good can be compared with God for goodness, so no evil can be compared with sin for evil."[9]

To elaborate further: "Sin is contrary to the names and attributes of God."[10] All that is in God (which is God)[11] in the fullness of His attributes is contrary to sin. Sin denies His all-sufficiency, because by it the sinner seeks satisfaction apart from contentment in God. "It challenges the justice of God and dares God to do His worst (Mal. 2:17). It provokes the Lord to jealousy and tempts Him to wrath."[12] Venning outlines specifically how sin is against God's omniscience, goodness, and grace. Sin in its very nature is the attempt to dethrone God as an affront to His sovereignty.[13] He continues, "Sin is contrary to the works of God…to the law and will of God…to the image of God…to the people and children of God…and set against the glory of God."[14] Every one of those points receives exposition in his masterful treatise.[15]

The Puritans viewed the gravity of sin in proportion to the infinitude of God's majesty. Since God is infinitely glorious, sin

---

to Ephesians 4:30, says, "This is spoken metaphorically. Sin is said to grieve the Spirit: because it is an injury offered to the Spirit, and he takes it unkindly, and, as it were, lays it to heart." *A Body of Divinity: Contained in Sermons Upon the Westminster Assembly's Catechism* (1692; repr., Edinburgh: Banner of Truth, 2012), 133.

8. Venning, *The Sinfulness of Sin*, 30.

9. Venning, *The Sinfulness of Sin*, 31.

10. Venning, *The Sinfulness of Sin*, 31.

11. There is nothing in God that is not His essence. This is just a way of stating the doctrine of divine simplicity, to which the Puritans held.

12. Venning, *The Sinfulness of Sin*, 32.

13. Venning, *The Sinfulness of Sin*, 31.

14. Venning, *The Sinfulness of Sin*, 32–35.

15. See also Joseph Alleine, *An Alarm to the Unconverted* (Lafayette, Ind.: Sovereign Grace Publishers, 2002), 58–61. Alleine (1634–1668) pleads with sinners to be converted and expounds on how all of God's attributes are opposed to them in the state of sin. It is enough to make any sober soul tremble!

is unspeakably heinous. Listen to John Bunyan: "No sin against God can be little, because it is against the great God of heaven and earth; but if the sinner can find out a little God, it may be easy to find out little sins."[16] The revelation of God's greatness and glory will expose the hideousness of sin, as it did in Isaiah 6 when the prophet was stricken with God's holiness and cried, "Woe is me."

What is your view of God? Do you have a big God, an infinite God, the God of Scripture? Then your sin will be a big deal to you, to say the least. The Puritans had a high view of the grace of God in salvation because they had a high view of sin, and they had a high view of sin because they had such a high view of God.

Sin in Relation to Man

Venning shows how sin is not only contrary to God but contrary also "to the good of man."[17] It is contrary to his body and soul, his rest and ease, his comfort and joy.[18] It has degraded man. "Man was a noble thing, made little lower than the angels (Ps. 8:5). But, alas, by sin he is made almost as low as devils."[19] Beyond this, it strips him of his eternal hope. Man was created with a "chief and ultimate end, the *summum bonum*,"[20] to glorify God and enjoy Him forever. But sin devastates that high calling. So perverse is the power of sin that it turns us all, in spite of God's clear revelation, into practical atheists. "Since sin, man has become such a fool as to say, in his heart, There is no God, at least no happiness in knowing God; for if sin does not make men such atheists as to believe there is no God, yet it makes them such as to wish there were no God, and to say that it is no happiness to know him."[21] What a tragedy!

---

16. John Bunyan, *Bunyan's Dying Sayings*, in *Works*, 1:65.
17. Venning, *The Sinfulness of Sin*, 37.
18. Venning, *The Sinfulness of Sin*, 38–42.
19. Venning, *The Sinfulness of Sin*, 44.
20. Venning, *The Sinfulness of Sin*, 51.
21. Venning, *The Sinfulness of Sin*, 52.

The Puritans held to an Augustinian doctrine of original sin in that they insisted on the fall and corruption of all humankind in Adam.[22] But they developed this doctrine more keenly as they understood it in light of covenant theology. They held to a historical Adam who by his transgression fell. "In Adam's fall, we sinned all," they affirmed. This is because Adam was a "public person" who represented his posterity in the covenant of works. His sin is imputed to those he represented (which is all humanity except for Christ, who was a distinct covenant Head; see Rom. 5:12–21), resulting in the inherent corruption of a pervasive depravity.

Thomas Goodwin (1600–1680) explains,

> We are arrested not only as guilty of that first cursed act which he personally performed, and so in regard of it are termed sinners, and exposed liable to God's wrath, but also as guilty of an universal, total, sinful defilement, spread over all faculties of soul and body, containing in it a privation or want of all good, and an inclination to all evil (which our Saviour Christ here, and the Scripture elsewhere, calls flesh), which is traduced unto us by birth and fleshly generation, "that which is born of the flesh is flesh," and which infects all mankind, even all that is said to be "born of flesh," all that is in man: "that which is born of the flesh is flesh."[23]

Among the faculties exposed to sin's reigning power is the mind. Romans 3:11 says that "there is none that understandeth." The noetic consequences of sin consist of the effects of the fall upon the thinking of the fallen. Venning says that sin "has dimmed and benighted man's leading faculty, the understanding, which should show a man the difference between good and evil, and

---

22. There are nuanced differences that are not pertinent to the present discussion. We are merely asserting, without going into specific details, that the Puritans stood in the Augustinian stream of the doctrines of sin and grace against all forms of Pelagianism.

23. Thomas Goodwin, *An Unregenerate Man's Guiltiness Before God, In Respect of Sin and Punishment,* in *The Works of Thomas Goodwin* (Edinburgh: James Nichol, 1865), 10:40–41.

guide him in the way in which he should walk. Now it is too often an *ignis fatuus* (will-o'-the-wisp) which leads men into bogs and ditches, into errors and immoralities."[24]

Sin in its exceeding sinfulness has a deceitful nature. The apostle John frequently portrays sin as "darkness" in his gospel account (John 1:5; 3:19; 8:12). It blinds the eyes so that sinners grope in darkness (1 John 2:11). The author to the Hebrews warns us not to be "hardened through the deceitfulness of sin" (Heb. 3:13). Sin corrupts the judgment and enslaves the will. Our rational faculties remain in place, but they turn corrupt as they employ themselves in the service of an affectional disposition that prefers the pleasure of sin. Rather than exposing sin, we hide it. Rather than confessing sin, we justify it. Fallen humanity is in love with sin and is at enmity with God.

The Puritans studied *hamartiology* (the doctrine of sin) and *anthropology* (the doctrine of man) deeply, in order to trace out the influences and effects of sin and to expose it for what it is. As Ferguson writes, "To them, systematic theology was to the pastor what anatomy is to the physician. Only in the light of the whole body of divinity (as they liked to call it) could a minister provide a diagnosis of, prescribe for, and ultimately cure spiritual disease in those who were plagued by the body of sin and death."[25]

People tend to flatter themselves with their own goodness and need to be awakened to the reality of sin. Even true believers are still susceptible to sin's deceitful influence. Though not under its power, the Christian is never freed from sin's presence in this life. Therefore, the Puritans believed, sinner and saint alike need to be jolted and awakened to the gravity of sin. To do this, the Puritans used many powerful arguments.

Many Puritans demonstrated sin's heinousness by pointing out its consequences for the One who is the epitome and perfection

---

24. Venning, *The Sinfulness of Sin*, 47.
25. Quoted in Joel R. Beeke, *Puritan Evangelism: A Biblical Approach* (Grand Rapids: Reformation Heritage Books), 15.

of humanity, the God-man Himself. That should be enough to melt the heart of any believer. Sin was imputed to the sinless One. The hell it incurred on that cursed tree reveals its true nature as it engulfed the spotless Lamb in the fury of God's almighty wrath. Redemption came at such a high cost, the cost of the precious blood of God's own Son, because nothing else could redeem from sin. John Flavel wrote,

> Is there any among us that make too light of sin, and are easily overcome by every temptation to the commission of it? O come hither, and "behold the Lamb of God!" and you cannot possibly have slight thoughts of sin after such a sight of Christ. See here the price of sin! behold what it cost the Lord Jesus Christ to expiate it. Did he come into the world as a Lamb, bound with the bands of an irreversible decree, to die for sin? Did he come from the bosom of the Father, to be our ransomer, and that at the price of his own life? Did the hand of severe justice shed the heart-blood of this immaculate Lamb, to satisfy for the wrongs thy sins have done to God? And yet, canst thou look upon sin as a light matter! God forbid![26]

Another line of argument the Puritans would use to expose sin's heinousness was by comparing it with the most unpleasant thing known to man: *suffering*. Thomas Watson said, "There is more evil in the least sin than in the greatest bodily evils that can befall us."[27] Jeremiah Burroughs (1600–1646) published an extensive treatise titled *The Evil of Evils*,[28] in which he argues with much specificity and many reasons that sin is worse than any other pain. "There is more evil in the least sin than in the greatest affliction."[29]

---

26. John Flavel, *Sacramental Meditations Upon Diverse Select Places of Scripture*, in *The Whole Works of the Reverend John Flavel* (London: W. Baynes and Son, 1820), 6:414–15.

27. Watson, *A Body of Divinity*, 136.

28. Jeremiah Burroughs, *The Evil of Evils* (1654; repr., Grand Rapids: Soli Deo Gloria, 2020).

29. Burroughs, *The Evil of Evils*, 24.

He argues that sin and God are contrary to each other, sin opposes all that is good, sin is the poison of all evils, sin bears an infinite dimension and character, and sin makes us comfortable with the devil.

Furthermore, God created hell to punish sin for the sake of vindicating His glory. We look upon sin with delight and get offended at the thought of an eternal hell. But hell doesn't offend God. Sin offends God. From God's perspective (which is the right one), the least sin is worse than the greatest suffering, including the agonies of hell.

Sin in Relation to the Christian

Though not freed from sin's influence, by the power of the gospel the believer has been freed from sin's dominion. Watson wrote, "A godly man doth not indulge himself in any sin. Though sin lives in him, yet he doth not live in sin."[30] There has been a radical reversal in the relationship the believer has with sin. Prior to conversion, sin was relished and practiced. Afterward, there is a striving against sin and a habitual victory over it. In Christ, those who love righteousness hate evil (Ps. 45:7). Emphasizing the sinfulness of sin has a sanctifying effect in its didactic function: it helps to stir up in our hearts more of an intense and holy hatred for sin. We can never hate sin enough. We need to learn to view it as God views it.

Part of viewing our sin correctly is understanding that our remaining sin pertains to our *condition* in this life, but such is not to be confused with our *position* in Christ. Thomas Watson issued these words of pastoral counsel to believers in his treatise on *The Mischief of Sin*:

> Here is a pillar of support to every soul who has broken off sin
> and espoused holiness. This is undoubted evidence that you

---

30. Thomas Watson, "The Godly Man's Picture Drawn with a Scripture-Pencil," in *Discourses on Important and Interesting Subjects, Being the Select Works of the Rev. Thomas Watson*, vol. 1 (Edinburgh: Blackie, Fullarton, 1829), 518.

are a true child of God. Flesh and blood could not reach to this, only omnipotent grace could conquer your corruption. 1 John 3:9, "He who is born of God doth not commit sin." He does not sin deliberately. He does not sin with delight. In his heart, he abhors sin; in his life, he forsakes it. Here is one who is born of God. And let this comfort the real penitent. Though he cannot get rid of a body of sin, but may have his failings do what he can, yet these failings shall not be charged upon him, but his Surety. God will be propitious through Christ. He will take notice of the sincerity and pass by the infirmity.[31]

Here we can see Watson balancing the truths of sanctification and justification. Sin has been broken off, but the believer still sins. "Yet these failings shall not be charged upon him, but [against] his Surety," the Lord Jesus Christ. Understanding the heinousness of sin spurs us on in our sanctification, but it also drives us further into Christ as we believe in Him for justification. Facing sin's exceeding sinfulness serves to foster deeper expressions of repentance as we abhor it, and it also serves to inspire greater measures of faith in the sufficiency of the blood of Christ that judicially removes it. In Adam, we inherit guilt and corruption; in Christ, we receive the twofold remedy of justification and sanctification. He removed the believer's *bad record* completely, and He is transforming the believer's *bad heart* progressively.

Holding the Tension in Balance

At the beginning of the chapter, we asked: How can we maintain a clean conscience if sin still remains in our consciousness? As believers, we must seek to convict our consciences of sin, but not as though we had no hope in Christ. That would only drive us to

---

31. Thomas Watson, *The Mischief of Sin* (1671; repr., Morgan, Pa.: Soli Deo Gloria, 1994), 79.

despair. We must do so within a gospel framework. Here are four directives that can help us do that.

1. Rest in the imputed righteousness of Christ. This is the key to securing a purified conscience. Hebrews 9:13–14 says, "For if the blood of bulls and of goats, and the ashes of an heifer sprinkling the unclean, sanctifieth to the purifying of the flesh: how much more shall the blood of Christ, who through the eternal Spirit offered himself without spot to God, purge your conscience from dead works to serve the living God?" The atonement satisfies for all our sin in all its blackness and filth. By faith, Christ becomes our perfect righteousness before the Father. We must trust in Him alone—not in our strivings against sin, not in our repentance, but in Christ. Don't think you must work up a certain level of abhorrence for sin before you can be commended to Christ for salvation and security. Venning counseled, "Prayers and tears, sighs and sorrows are not our savior; it is Jesus only who saves from sin."[32] The clearer sights you obtain of sin, the tighter you should cling to Christ alone as your sole confidence before God.

2. Practice daily self-examination in prayer and meditation. In our busy and hurried lives, we give little thought to the inner workings of conscience. What poor listeners we are to our poor consciences! We need to tune out all of the distracting noise around us and get alone in the presence of God regularly. We need to study God's Word, yes, but we also need to study our hearts. Watson said, "Self-searching is heart-anatomy. A surgeon, when he makes a dissection in the body, discovers the inward parts, the heart, the liver, and arteries; so a Christian anatomizes himself; he searches what is flesh and what is spirit, what is sin and what is grace."[33] As we reflect back on the previous day, week, month, and year, let us probe

---

32. Venning, *The Sinfulness of Sin*, 220.
33. Thomas Watson, *Heaven Taken by Storm* (1669; repr., Orlando, Fla.: Northhampton Press, 2007), 36.

our consciences with the Scriptures. This will help us to discern our faults, but it will also enable us to confess them for cleansing (1 John 1:9), to watch over our hearts and guard them (Prov. 4:23), and to pray for strength by the supply of the Spirit to help us in our weakness (Matt. 6:13).

3. Endeavor to procure a tender conscience, and once procured, cherish it with great care. "Keep a tender conscience, which will not make light of sin," counsels Richard Baxter (1615–1691).[34] A tender conscience is precious in the sight of God. Easily pricked by the thorn of besetting sin, it spurs a person to keep short accounts with God.[35] Thomas Manton (1620–1677) explained: "This is the difference between a tender conscience and a hard heart—one is afraid to offend God in the least matter, the other makes nothing of sin, and so runneth into mischief, Prov. 28:14. Well, then, a man that hath a tender heart is loath to fall into the least sin, he is ever drawing to God to be kept from all sin. When we are earnest in this matter, it is a sign we are sensible what an evil sin is."[36] A tender conscience will keep you nearer to God, the fount of all joy and assurance.

4. Expose sin to your consciousness fully and repent of it deeply. Don't spare yourself by playing favorites with "Number One." Beware of partiality in dealing with your sin that would arise from the bias of self-preference or self-love. Thomas Watson said, "The devil would paint sin with the vermilion colour of pleasure and profit, that he may make it look fair; but I shall pull off the paint that you may see its ugly face. We are apt to have slight thoughts of sin."[37]

---

34 Richard Baxter, *The Practical Works of the Rev. Richard Baxter* (London: James Duncan, 1830), 6:385.

35. A tender conscience is not to be confused with a weak conscience. I am commending a biblically informed, healthy, sensitive conscience. Such a conscience will fear unlawful things rather than viewing lawful things with trepidation.

36. Thomas Manton, *Several Sermons Upon the CXIX. Psalm,* in *The Complete Works of Thomas Manton* (London: James Nisbet, 1872), 8:203.

37. Watson, *A Body of Divinity*, 132.

Meditate on the evil of sin, on God's attributes in opposition to it, and on Calvary's cross in the light of it. Don't sweep it under the rug; own it, fess up to it in the presence of God, bring it before the face of your conscience, grieve over it, renounce it by name, repent of it particularly, and determine with all holy resolution to depart from it. Reflect on what may occasion or aggravate your sin, and target these weaknesses in prayer as well. Read Thomas Watson's helpful book, *The Doctrine of Repentance*,[38] and pray earnestly that the Lord would work such a thorough and abiding repentance into the depths of your heart.

Trusting in Christ as our righteousness, practicing daily self-examination, maintaining a tender conscience, and repenting deeply of sin will help us to maintain pure consciences in the light of sin's exceeding sinfulness. The purpose of dwelling on this topic is not so that we may endlessly grovel in our own misery but so that we may gain a greater experiential acquaintance with the greatness of the grace that deals with our sin. The power of sin points us by the gospel to the even greater power of Christ.

In Christ, it is possible to enjoy the sweet assurance of a peaceful conscience. Put the biblical counsel of the Puritans into practice and you will see! Watson proclaimed, "O the music of conscience! Conscience is turned into a paradise, and there a Christian sweetly solaces himself and plucks the flowers of joy."[39] As we grow in our experiential acquaintance with sin's sinfulness (since with sanctification comes a growing sensitivity to sin), let us also seek to cultivate and grow in assurance. That is the Puritan way.

---

38. Thomas Watson, *The Doctrine of Repentance* (1668; repr., Edinburgh: Banner of Truth, 2012).

39. Watson, *The Doctrine of Repentance*, 98.

Questions for Reflection and Discussion

1. Before reading this chapter, had you seriously considered how sin offends God? People often grieve over the personal consequences of sin, without giving much thought to the Godward dimension of sin. How has this chapter helped you better understand David's words, "Against thee, thee only, have I sinned and done this evil in thy sight" (Ps. 51:4)?

2. How do you usually deal with a guilty conscience? Do you ignore, excuse, or rationalize sin? Or have you learned to turn from sin, while taking refuge in Christ's obedience, righteousness, and grace?

3. Is your conscience tender or hardened? Reflect for a few moments: when was the last time you were convicted of unholy thoughts or motives? When was the last time you confessed your sins to the Lord in prayer? Do you respond to the Spirit's conviction with swift repentance?

4

THE PURITANS
Open Our Eyes to the Beauty
and Loveliness of Christ

We can preach nothing else as the object of our faith…only Christ is the whole of man's happiness, the Sun to enlighten him, the Physician to heal him, the Wall of fire to defend him, the Friend to comfort him, the Pearl to enrich him, the Ark to support him, the Rock to sustain him under the heaviest pressures…. As Christ is more excellent than all the world, so this sight transcends all other sights; it is the epitome of a Christian's happiness, the quintessence of evangelical duties, Looking unto JESUS.

—ISAAC AMBROSE[1]

The Puritans were as Christ-centered as they were God-centered. They loved Christ passionately and sought His glory tirelessly. Christ meant everything to them.

Richard Sibbes, in a funeral sermon on Philippians 1:23–24, expressed a common Puritan sentiment: "Heaven is not heaven without Christ. It is better to be in any place with Christ than to be in heaven itself without him. All delicacies without Christ are but as a funeral banquet…. What is all without Christ? I say the

1. Isaac Ambrose, *Looking Unto Jesus: A View of the Everlasting Gospel, or, The Soul's Eyeing of Jesus, As Carrying on the Great Work of Man's Salvation from First to Last* (Philadelphia: J. B. Lippincott, 1856), 17–18.

joys of heaven are not the joys of heaven without Christ; he is the very heaven of heaven."[2] The Puritans saw Christ on virtually every page of Scripture. Thomas Adams (1583–1652) wrote, "Christ is the sole paragon of our joy, the fountain of life, the foundation of all blessedness. Christ is the sum of the whole Bible, prophesied, typified, prefigured, exhibited, demonstrated, to be found in every leaf, almost in every line, the Scriptures being but as it were the swaddling bands of the child Jesus."[3] Nor was Adams alone, for the Puritans left behind dozens of sermons, discourses, treatises, and even personal letters that show their bright faith and burning love for Jesus Christ.

In this chapter, we will see how the Puritans can help us better glorify and enjoy Christ by considering three things: (1) meditation on Christ's person and work; (2) communion with Christ in His grace; and (3) satisfaction in Christ's sufficiency, loveliness, and beauty.

Meditation on Christ's Person and Work

One of the best examples of devotional meditation on Christ is *Looking Unto Jesus* by Isaac Ambrose (1604–1664). Occasioned by his own experience following a terrible sickness in 1653, Ambrose began to think of the many things Jesus had done for his soul, tracing His work back to God's gracious eternal plan and forward to future glory. "I could find no beginning of his actings, but in that eternity before the world was made," Ambrose wrote, "nor could I find any end of his actions, but in that eternity after the world should be unmade: only between these two extremities, I apprehended various transactions of Jesus Christ, both past, present and to come."[4] In his meditations, Ambrose "found a world of

---

2. Richard Sibbes, *Christ is Best* (Edinburgh: Banner of Truth, 2012), 11.
3. Thomas Adams, "Meditations upon the Creed," in *The Works of Thomas Adams* (1862; repr. Eureka, Calif.: Tanski, 1998), 3:224.
4. Ambrose, *Looking Unto Jesus*, vii.

spiritual comfort" in both the act of looking to Christ and in Christ Himself, the object of his meditations.[5]

Ambrose called looking unto Jesus "the duty of duties, the chief duty, the especial duty"—in fact, the "essential part" in all other duties, since "it is only from Christ that virtue and efficacy is communicated in spiritual ordinances."[6] The duty Ambrose had in mind is "the look of our minds and hearts, whereby we not only see spiritual things, but we are affected with them."[7] The act of looking, therefore, includes the acts of "knowing, considering, desiring, hoping, believing, loving, joying, enjoying of Jesus, and conforming [ourselves] to Jesus."[8]

The range of material Ambrose covered is impressive, including the full sweep of redemptive history. But throughout, Ambrose maintained his steadfast focus on Jesus. "Only Christ," wrote Ambrose, "is the sun and centre of all divine revealed truths":

> We can preach nothing else as the object of our faith, as the necessary element of your soul's salvation, which doth not some way or other, either meet in Christ, or refer to Christ; only Christ is the whole of man's happiness, the Sun to enlighten him, the Physician to heal him, the Wall of fire to defend him, the Friend to comfort him, the Pearl to enrich him, the Ark to support him, the Rock to sustain him under the heaviest pressures.... As Christ is more excellent than all the world, so this sight transcends all other sights; it is the epitome of a Christian's happiness, the quintessence of evangelical duties, Looking unto JESUS.[9]

In the course of his book, Ambrose directs the believer's focus to the eternal foundations of our salvation in sovereign election and the "great treaty betwixt God and Christ," as well as the covenant

---

5. Ambrose, *Looking Unto Jesus,* vii.
6. Ambrose, *Looking Unto Jesus,* 36.
7. Ambrose, *Looking Unto Jesus,* 26.
8. Ambrose, *Looking Unto Jesus,* 28.
9. Ambrose, *Looking Unto Jesus,* 17–18.

promise of Christ manifested to Adam, Abraham, Moses, David, and Israel. He expounds the great work of redemption from the creation until Christ's first coming, and then the tidings, conception, natures, birth, baptism, temptation, and earthly ministry of Christ.

Then (some 325 pages in!), Ambrose concentrates more directly on the sufferings of Christ, dividing His passion into "its parts and hours," leading through His trials and up to His death. Next, Ambrose turns to the resurrection and its time, reasons, manner, arguments, and appearances; Christ's ascension to the right hand of God, along with His session, intercession, and the sending of the Spirit; and, finally, Christ's second coming in judgment and salvation.

In all these aspects of Christ's saving work, Ambrose seeks to direct his readers to know, consider, desire, hope, believe, love, rejoice in, call upon, and conform themselves to Jesus.[10] "There are many glorious sights in Jesus,"[11] Ambrose said, and his invitation to his readers reveals the heartfelt devotion with which he wrote: "I beseech thee, come warm thy heart at this blessed fire! O! come, 'and smell the precious ointments of Jesus Christ!' O! come, 'and sit under his shadow with great delight!' oh! that all men…would presently fall upon the practice of this gospel art of 'looking unto Jesus.' "[12]

Ambrose was certainly not the only Puritan to practice this gospel art of looking unto Jesus. Christ-centered meditation of this sort was a common feature in the sermons of the Puritans as a whole. William Bridge (1600–1670), for example, called Christ "the great Lord-Keeper of His Father's wardrobe,"[13] that is, the

---

10. Ambrose, *Looking Unto Jesus,* xi–xvi.

11. Ambrose, *Looking Unto Jesus,* 44.

12. Ambrose, *Looking Unto Jesus,* ix.

13. William Bridge, *Grace for Grace, or the Overflowings of Christ's Fulness received by all Saints,* in *The Works of the Reverend William Bridge* (1845; repr., Beaver Falls, Pa.: Soli Deo Gloria, 1989), 1:262.

sole administrator through whom God dispenses grace to His people. Bridge beckoned his hearers to consider the many metaphors used in Scripture to set forth Christ to the souls of His people:

> Cast your eyes where you will, you shall hardly look upon any thing, but Jesus Christ hath taken that name upon himself. If you cast your eyes up to heaven in the day, and behold the sun, he is called "the Sun of Righteousness" (Mal. 4:2). If you cast your eyes in the night upon the stars, or in the morning upon the morning star, he is called "the bright Morning Star" (Rev. 22:16). If you behold your own body, he is called the head, and the church the body (Col. 1:18). If you look upon your own clothes, he is called your raiment: "Put ye on the Lord Jesus" (Rom. 13:14). If you behold your meat, he is called bread, "the Bread of Life" (John 6:35). If you look upon your houses, he is called a door (John 10:9). If you look abroad into the fields, and behold the cattle of the fields, he is called the Good Shepherd (John 10:11); he is called the Lamb (John 1:29); he is called the fatted calf (Luke 15:23). If you look upon the waters, he is called a fountain; the blood of Christ a fountain (Zech. 13:1). If you look upon the stones, he is called "a Corner Stone" (Isa. 28:16). If you look upon the trees, he is called "a Tree of Life" (Prov. 3:18). What is the reason for this? Surely, not only to way-lay your thoughts, that wheresoever you look, still you should think of Christ; but to show, that in a spiritual way and sense, he is all this unto the soul.[14]

Still other examples include *Christ All in All* by Philip Henry (1631–1696) (father of the famous commentator Matthew Henry),[15] John Flavel's *Fountain of Life*,[16] Thomas Goodwin's trilogy of books

---

14. Bridge, *Grace for Grace,* in *Works,* 1:262.

15. Philip Henry, *Christ All in All: What Christ Is Made to Believers* (Grand Rapids: Soli Deo Gloria, 2016)

16. John Flavel, *The Fountain of Life Opened Up, or a Display of Christ in His Essential and Mediatorial Glory*, in *The Works of John Flavel* (1820; repr., Edinburgh: Banner of Truth, 1968), 1:1–561.

on Christ—*Christ Set Forth, The Heart of Christ in Heaven,* and *Christ the Mediator*[17]; and John Owen's final book, *Meditations and Discourses on the Glory of Christ.*[18]

These are just a few examples showing how the Puritans fostered meditation on Christ by covering the whole terrain of His person, natures, offices, states, names, titles, and mediatorial work—including His life, ministry, death, resurrection, ascension, session, intercession, and second coming.

Communion with Christ in His Grace

The Christ-centeredness of the Puritans is also evident in their teaching on communion with Christ.

In his theological and devotional masterpiece, *Of Communion with God the Father, Son, and Holy Ghost, Each Person Distinctly in Love, Grace, and Consolation,* John Owen describes the believer's communion with Christ in terms of "purchased grace," which he defines as "all that righteousness and grace which Christ has procured or wrought for us and of which he makes us partakers."[19] Owen then breaks this down into three categories: (1) "the grace

---

17. Thomas Goodwin, *Christ Set Forth* in *The Works of Thomas Goodwin,* ed. Thomas Smith (1861–1866; repr., Grand Rapids: Reformation Heritage Books, 2006), 4:1–91; *The Heart of Christ in Heaven* in *Works,* 4:93–150; and *Christ the Mediator* in *Works,* 5:1–496. See also Joel R. Beeke and Mark Jones, eds., *"A Habitual Sight of Him": The Christ-Centered Piety of Thomas Goodwin* (Grand Rapids: Reformation Heritage Books, 2009) and "Thomas Goodwin on Christ's Beautiful Heart" in Joel R. Beeke and Mark Jones, *A Puritan Theology: Doctrine for Life* (Grand Rapids: Reformation Heritage Books, 2012), 387–99.

18. John Owen, *Meditations and Discourses on the Glory of Christ,* in *The Works of John Owen,* ed. W. H. Gould (1850–1853; repr., Edinburgh: Banner of Truth, 1966), 1:273–415.

19. John Owen, *Communion with God: Abridged and Made Easy to Read* by R. J. K. Law (Edinburgh: Banner of Truth, 1991). This modernized abridgment (hereafter Law, *Communion with God*) in Banner of Truth's series of Puritan Paperback makes Owen more accessible to contemporary readers. I will also include references (and at times quotes) from the original in Owen's *Works.* For this quotation, see John Owen, *Of Communion with God* in *The Works of John Owen,* ed. W. H. Goold (1850–1853; repr., Edinburgh: Banner of Truth, 1966), 2:154.

of justification or acceptance with God," (2) "the grace of sanctification or holiness before God," and (3) "the grace of privilege."[20] The foundation of this purchased grace is found in Christ's obedient life, sacrificial death, and heavenly intercession as our Mediator. Owen's meditations on these glorious aspects of Christ's work penetrate deep into the heart of biblical truth. But here I especially want to highlight his pastoral application to the daily life of the believer.

In showing how the believer applies the purchased grace of acceptance with God, Owen explains two requirements. First, we must "heartily approve of this righteousness as purchased by him so that we might be accepted by God."[21] To wholeheartedly embrace Christ's righteousness presupposes a deep conviction that righteousness is necessary if we are to appear before God—and that our own righteousness is utterly lacking. Then, persuaded of our desperate need, we are prepared to value the provision of Christ's complete and perfect righteousness as full of infinite wisdom and grace, and as the only way of securing peace for our souls.

Furthermore, we approve of this righteousness because it brings maximum glory to God: "When [believers] were under the guilt of sin, they were puzzled as to how they could be saved and God's justice, faithfulness and truth glorified. Believers see that, by this righteousness, all the properties of God are greatly glorified in the pardon, justification, and acceptance of sinners."[22]

This leads to the second requirement: not only must we embrace and approve of this righteousness, but we must "make an actual commutation," or exchange, "with the Lord Jesus."[23] This

---

20. Law, *Communion with God*, 118; Owen, *Of Communion with God*, in *Works, Works*, 2:155.

21. Law, *Communion with God*, 141; Owen, *Of Communion with God*, in *Works*, 2:187.

22. Law, *Communion with God*, 143; Owen, *Of Communion with God*, in *Works*, 2:193.

23. Owen, *Of Communion with God*, in *Works*, 2:193. Law unfortunately does not paraphrase this important sentence from Owen. Law also dispenses with the

involves keeping the sense of sin's guilt and evil alive in our hearts, bringing our particular sins to God in prayer, and fixing our faith upon Christ. Believers thus "lay down their sins at the cross of Christ, upon his shoulders." Owen continues,

> This is faith's great and bold venture upon the grace, faithfulness, and truth of God, to stand by the cross and say, "Ah! he is bruised for my sins, and wounded for my transgressions, and the chastisement of my peace is upon him. He is thus made sin for me. Here I give up my sins to him that is able to bear them, to undergo them. He requires it of my hands, that I should be content that he should undertake for them; and that I heartily consent unto." This is every day's work; I know not how any peace can be maintained without it.... [This is] to know Christ crucified.
>
> Having thus by faith given up their sins to Christ, and seen God laying them all on him, they draw nigh and take from him that righteousness which he has wrought out for them; so fulfilling the whole of that of the apostle, 2 Cor. 5:21, "He was made sin for us, that we might be made the righteousness of God in him." They consider him tendering himself and his righteousness, to be their righteousness before God; they take it, and accept of it, and complete this blessed bartering and exchange of faith. Anger, curse, wrath, death, sin as to its guilt, he took it all and takes it all away. With him we leave whatever of this nature belongs to us; and from him we receive love, life, righteousness, and peace. [24]

Owen then answers two possible objections. First, a believer might object that this arrangement could never be acceptable to Christ. "Shall we daily come to him with our filth, our guilt, our sins? Will he not tell us to keep them ourselves? Shall we always

---

numbers outlining Owen's points. Although this makes it somewhat easier to read Owen, there is a corresponding loss in terms of the clarity and structure of Owen's full argument.

24. Owen, *Of Communion with God,* in *Works,* 2:194; See also Law, *Communion with God,* 144.

be giving him our sins and taking his righteousness?"[25] Owen answers by showing that this blessed exchange is not only acceptable to Christ but delights and honors Him: "There is nothing that Jesus Christ is more delighted with than that his saints should always hold communion with him by giving him their sins and receiving his righteousness. This greatly honors him and gives him the glory that is his due."[26]

The second objection concerns antinomianism: "If this is so, why do we need to repent and amend our ways? Why not go on sinning, so that grace may abound?"[27] In answer, Owen appeals to Paul's answer to the same objection in Romans 6:1–3 and argues that genuine communion with Christ produces both gospel repentance (with a godly sorrow for sin) and obedience to God.

In his book on temptation, Owen also highlights the practical value of daily communion with Christ, but now as the primary means of preserving the soul from temptations to sin. "He who makes it his business to eat daily of the tree of life will have no appetite for the other fruit, even if the tree that bears them seems to stand in the midst of paradise," Owen writes. "Let a soul, then, exercise itself to a communion with Christ in the good things of the gospel, the pardon of sin, the fruits of holiness, the hope of glory, peace with God, joy in the Holy Spirit, dominion over sin, and it shall have a powerful protection against all temptations."[28]

---

25. Law, *Communion with God*, 144; Owen, *Of Communion with God*, in *Works*, 2:195.

26. Law, *Communion with God*, 144–45; Owen, *Of Communion with God*, in *Works*, 2:195.

27. Law, *Communion with God*, 145; Owen, *Of Communion with God*, in *Works*, 2:196.

28. Owen, *Temptation Resisted and Repulsed* (Edinburgh: Banner of Truth, 2007), 102. See also *Of Temptation*, in *The Works of John Owen*, ed. W. H. Goold (1850–1853; repr., Edinburgh: Banner of Truth, 1966), 6:144.

Satisfaction in Christ's Sufficiency, Loveliness, and Beauty

The result of real, vital, personal communion with the Lord Jesus Christ is deep satisfaction and joy in Him, resulting in wonder, love, and praise. Thriving in grace is, essentially, just this: a growing satisfaction in the sufficiency, loveliness, and beauty of Christ. Owen wrote,

> I have had more advantage by private thoughts of Christ than by anything in this world, and I think when a soul hath satisfying and exalting thoughts of Christ himself, his person and his glory, it is the way whereby Christ dwells in such a soul. If I have observed anything by personal experience, it is this,—a man may take the measure of his growth and decay in grace according to his thoughts and meditations upon the person of Christ, and the glory of Christ's kingdom, and his love. A heart that is inclined to converse with Christ as he is represented in the gospel, is a thriving heart; and if estranged from it and backward to it, it is under deadness and decays.[29]

This theme—satisfaction in the all-sufficient beauty and loveliness of Jesus Christ—finds constant expression in the Puritans. But what does it mean to say that Christ is all-sufficient, and why does it matter? It means that Christ in all of His fullness really is everything we need. And it matters because without Him we can do nothing.

To say that Christ is sufficient is to say that there is nothing else in addition to Jesus that we need for salvation, life, satisfaction, or fullness. There are no bonuses or extras. There is no gold membership to be attained only by an elite few. If Christ really is sufficient, then Christianity can do without the extra "-isms": legalism, mysticism, Gnosticism, asceticism, monasticism, sacerdotalism, and so on—"-isms," we should note, against which the Puritans often set forth their positive expositions of gospel truth.

---

29. Owen, "The Excellency of Christ," in *Works,* 9:475.

We can go even further. The claim that Christ is sufficient means not only that we need no additions to Jesus, but also that any such additions are actually subtractions. To try to add something to Christ's finished work is to diminish what He has already done. If you say that you need Christ plus angels, or Christ plus the law, or Christ plus moral achievement, or Christ plus a second work of grace, or Christ plus anything else—then you take something away from Christ (see especially Col. 2:6–23). To say that Christ is sufficient is to say that the God and Father of our Lord Jesus Christ has *already* blessed us in Christ with every spiritual blessing in the heavenly places (Eph. 1:3–14). To say that Christ is sufficient is to say that God has already given us everything we need for life and godliness through His own Son (2 Peter 1:3). To say that Christ is sufficient is to say that the only thing the branch needs in order to bear fruit is to be connected vitally to the vine (John 15:1–8).

But the declaration that Christ is sufficient should not make us complacent. We must be careful to not draw the wrong conclusions or make the wrong applications. The completeness of Christ's work does not mean that we have no needs. It means that all of the needs we have are met in Christ—and that, therefore, we must seek Him!

The doctrine of Christ's sufficiency, rightly understood, will never allow us to rest content in spiritual ignorance. "No man can receive Jesus Christ in the darkness of natural ignorance," wrote John Flavel. "We must understand and discern who and what he is, whom we receive to be the Lord our righteousness. If we know not his person and his offices, we do not take, but mistake Christ."[30] We need to know the truths about Christ, because we need Him in all of His fullness. In one of his sermons, William Bridge argued that "all our want [lack] of comfort doth arise from our want of a

---

30. John Flavel, *The Method of Grace in the Gospel Redemption*, in *The Works of John Flavel* (1820; repr., Edinburgh: Banner of Truth, 1998), 2:106.

sight of the fullness and excellency that is in Christ."[31] Therefore, the way to greater comfort and joy is to see more of Christ.

We need not half a Christ, but the whole Christ.[32] We need the authentic Christ in all of His humble humanity and awe-inspiring deity. We need Jesus in His meekness and majesty, His suffering and glory, His crucifixion and resurrection, His incarnation and ascension, His first coming and His second. We need Jesus in His redeeming, liberating grace. We need His forgiveness for our sins, His cleansing for our consciences, and His power for our obedience. We need Christ in His supremacy over all earthly and unearthly powers, whether those powers are angels, principalities, and powers in the heavenly realms or Caesars, senators, and presidents in the kingdoms of men. We need Christ as the perfect portrait of the invisible God, as the true image of God, the new and better Adam, and as the greater son of David who in the strength of weakness sets His people free from the monsters of sin and death. We need Christ as justifier and sanctifier. We need Him as the Savior and Lord of the church, the husband of the bride, and the head of the body. We need Him as Lion of the tribe of Judah and as the Lamb that was slain from the foundation of the world. We need Him as prophet, priest, and king. We need him as bread of life and the fountain of living waters.[33] We need him as the door to walk through, the way to walk forward, and the goal to which

---

31. Bridge, "The Fullness of Christ," in *Works,* 5:25.

32. As Calvin said, "Christ cannot be torn into parts, so these two which we perceive in him together and conjointly are inseparable—namely, righteousness and sanctification." John Calvin, *Institutes of the Christian Religion,* ed. John T. McNeill, trans. Ford Lewis Battles (Philadelphia: Westminster Press, 1960), 3.11.6. Put another way, one cannot receive Jesus as Savior without also receiving him as Lord, nor can we separate the benefits that Christ gives from Christ himself. For more on this, see Sinclair B. Ferguson, *The Whole Christ: Legalism, Antinomianism & Gospel Assurance—Why the Marrow Controversy Still Matters* (Wheaton, Ill.: Crossway, 2016).

33. To quote Flavel again, Christ is "bread to the hungry, water to the thirsty, a garment to the naked, healing to the wounded, and whatever a soul can desire is found in him." *Method of Grace,* in *Works,* 2:216.

we walk; the prize for which we run; and the Captain for whom we fight. We need Christ as Alpha and Omega, beginning and end, first and last.

Furthermore, we need Jesus in all of life. We need Jesus informing our minds, and we need Jesus transforming and reforming our hearts. We need Jesus in the closet, the bedroom, the dining room, the playroom, the boardroom, and on the street. We need Jesus when we play, when we worship, when we work, and when we pray. We need Jesus in our churches, our classrooms, and our homes. We need Jesus in and through all the vicissitudes of life. We need Jesus to remove the burden of sin at Calvary and to strengthen us for the long pilgrimage to the Celestial City. We need Jesus to walk with us through the Valley of Humiliation. We need Him to help us make the hard climb up Hill Difficulty. We need Him to pull us from the Slough of Despond and to rescue us from Doubting Castle. We need Jesus for singleness, marriage, parenting, empty-nesting, and grandparenting. We need Him during college and career, at home and abroad, in our waking and in our sleeping, in our living and in our dying. In all that we are, we need all that He is. Our need is great. But His sufficiency is greater. The whole of Scripture proclaims the sufficiency of Christ as it unfolds the Father's plan to redeem His people and restore the world through the all-sufficient work of His Son and the power of His life-giving Spirit. If the whole of Scripture is a symphony, this is its melodic theme.

This theme set the Puritans' hearts on fire with love for Christ. This is one of the most compelling reasons we should continue to read them today. The Puritans will help you to see, love, honor, obey, glorify, and enjoy Christ more.

Perhaps no one has said this better than the Scottish Presbyterian Samuel Rutherford (1600–1661), whose letters, like the needle of a compass, consistently point to Christ as the True North of our soul's deepest desires. We conclude, then, with one well-known example from Rutherford:

This soul of ours hath love, and cannot but love some fair one; and O what a fair One, what an only One, what an excellent, lovely One is Jesus! Put the beauty of ten thousand thousand worlds of paradises like the garden of Eden in one; put all trees, all flowers, all smells, all colours, all tastes, all joys, all sweetness, all loveliness in one. O what a fair and excellent thing that would be! And yet it would be less, to that fair and dearest Well-beloved, Christ, than one drop of rain to the whole seas, rivers, lakes and fountains of ten thousand earths. O, but Christ is heaven's wonder, and earth's wonder! What marvel that his bride saith, "He is altogether lovely!"[34]

Questions for Reflection and Discussion

1. Have you learned "the gospel art" of looking unto Jesus, as described by Isaac Ambrose? How do you think such a focus on Christ should work out in practice? What would it look like in your daily life?

2. Did this chapter introduce you to any aspects of Christ's sufficiency that were new to you? How does seeing Christ's beauty draw your heart into wonder, love, and praise?

3. Reflect on Owen's description of communion with Christ in "purchased grace" through daily exchanging our sins for His righteousness. Does this characterize your own walk with Christ? If not, how would adopting this practice change you?

---

34. Samuel Rutherford, *Letters of Samuel Rutherford: A Selection* (Edinburgh: Banner of Truth, 1973), 120.

5

THE PURITANS
Liberate Our Hearts with the Freedom and Power of Grace

There is an infinite treasury of grace and holiness in Jesus Christ. This he hath not received for himself, but for others. There is an infinite propension [propensity] and willingness in him to give out this grace unto the children of men. And nothing either in heaven or earth can hinder him: surely therefore, there is the communication of fulness of Jesus Christ unto all believers.

—WILLIAM BRIDGE[1]

In one of his beloved letters, Samuel Rutherford said that "the freedom of grace and salvation is the wonder of man and angels."[2] Few truths have greater power to liberate our hearts than the doctrines of God's free and sovereign grace. Without grace, there could be no justification, no sanctification, and no glorification. Apart from grace, every man, woman, and child, from all times and places, would be utterly and fatally lost. Our redemption, from first to last, is all of grace. To quote Spurgeon, grace is the "golden thread" that runs "through the whole of the Christian's

1. William Bridge, *Grace for Grace, or the Overflowings of Christ's Fulness received by all Saints,* in *The Works of the Reverend William Bridge* (London: Thomas Tegg, 1845; repr. Beaver Falls, Pa.: Soli Deo Gloria Publications, 1989), 1:211.

2. Samuel Rutherford, *Letters of Samuel Rutherford: A Selection* (Edinburgh: Banner of Truth, 1973), 73.

history, from his election before all worlds, even to his admission to the heaven of rest."[3]

But while God's grace is truly marvelous and amazing, it is frequently misunderstood, often abused, and even denied.

To explain,[4] let me borrow and adapt an image from *The Pilgrim's Regress*, a magnificent allegory by C. S. Lewis (1898–1963).[5] If you think of the Christian life as a journey across a rugged terrain, there are significant dangers both to the north and to the south. To the frozen north are the arctic dangers of icy legalism and frigid formalism, where religiosity and self-righteousness freeze the heart, leaving us brittle, cold, and hard toward both God and fellow human beings.

But to the swampy south, there are the tropical dangers of sultry self-indulgence and lazy licentiousness, where grace is twisted into license, where holiness and obedience are neglected, and where biblically warranted, faith-fueled effort is condemned as legalism. Dietrich Bonhoeffer (1906–1945) famously called this "cheap grace,"[6] but the Puritans, more appropriately, called it "antinomianism" (which means "against law").

The church veers north when she loses her wonder at the *freedom* of grace, when the heart-warming doctrines of grace and of justification by faith alone slip from her grasp. But the church wanders south when she loses her wonder at the *power* of grace;

---

3. Charles H. Spurgeon, "Salvation All of Grace," in *The Metropolitan Tabernacle Pulpit Sermons* (London: Passmore & Alabaster, 1872; repr. Pasadena, Tex.: Pilgrim Publications, 1971), 18: 433.

4. The following three paragraphs are adapted from Brian G. Hedges, *Active Spirituality: Grace and Effort in the Christian Life* (Wapwallopen, Pa.: Shepherd Press, 2014), 10. Used with permission.

5. *The Pilgrim's Regress* was the first book C. S. Lewis wrote as a Christian and is both one of his most brilliant and most difficult books. The North and South for Lewis represented the philosophical dangers of overemphasizing objectivity and the intellect, on the one hand, and sentimentality and the emotions on the other. I've obviously adapted the imagery for theological purposes.

6. Dietrich Bonhoeffer, *The Cost of Discipleship* (New York: Collier Books, Macmillan Publishing Company, 1963 Revised Edition), 47.

neglects the biblical demands for effort, perseverance, and watchfulness; and collapses the action-laden language of the New Testament (walk, fight, run, conquer, etc.) into overly simplistic, reductionist formulas that vacate sanctifying faith of all effort. While the doctrines of grace and justification by faith alone rescue us from the frozen glacier of legalism, the doctrines of regeneration, sanctification, and the perseverance of the saints preserve us from the miry bog of antinomianism.

The church, in other words, must keep a firm grasp on what John Calvin called a double grace. "Christ was given to us by God's generosity," Calvin wrote, "to be grasped and possessed by us in faith. By partaking of him, we principally receive a double grace: namely, that being reconciled to God through Christ's blamelessness, we may have in heaven instead of a Judge a gracious Father; and secondly, that sanctified by Christ's spirit we may cultivate blamelessness and purity of life."[7] In this chapter, we will show that the Puritans were both articulate and persuasive in their exultant expositions of the freedom and power of God's grace.

The Freedom of God's Grace

Grace, by definition, is free. Grace is God's unmerited favor, freely bestowed on the unworthy. The Scriptures repeatedly set salvation by grace in opposition to salvation by works. "For by grace are ye saved through faith; and that not of yourselves: it is the gift of God: Not of works, lest any man should boast" (Eph. 2:8–9). "And if by grace, then is it no more of works: otherwise grace is no more grace. But if it be of works, then is it no more grace: otherwise work is no more work" (Rom. 11:6). To quote Rutherford again, "Grace, grace, free grace, the merits of Christ for nothing—must be the rock that we drowned souls must swim to."[8]

7. John Calvin, *Institutes of the Christian Religion*, ed. John T. McNeil, trans. Ford Lewis Battles (Philadelphia: Westminster Press, 1960), 3.11.1.
8. Rutherford, *Letters of Samuel Rutherford: A Selection,* 130.

1. Justified by Grace Alone, through Faith Alone. The freedom of God's grace was a regular feature in Puritan theology, seen especially in their expositions of the doctrine of justification. One of the best examples is *Justification Vindicated* by Robert Traill (1642–1716), a short book originally written in 1692 to Traill's brother William, minister of Borthwick, Midlothian, to defend "the good old way of the Protestant doctrine" of justification by faith alone from the errors of both Neonomianism and Antinomianism.[9]

Traill argues that the

> doctrine of the justification of a sinner by the free grace of God in Jesus Christ, however it may be misrepresented and reproached, is yet undeniably recommended by four things:

> 1. It is a doctrine savoury and precious to all serious, godly persons.

> 2. It is that doctrine only by which a convinced sinner can be dealt with effectually.

> 3. This doctrine of free justification by faith alone has this advantage, that it suits all men's spirits and frames in their serious approaches to God in worship.

> 4. This doctrine of justification by faith without any mixtures of man (by whatever names and titles they may be dignified or distinguished) has this undoubted advantage, that it is that to which all not judicially hardened and blinded do, or would, or must, betake themselves when dying.[10]

Occasioned by the antinomian controversy, following the published writings of Tobias Crisp (1600–1643), Traill clearly and persuasively defends the Protestant doctrine of justification on the basis of Christ's imputed righteousness, through the

---

9. See Joel R. Beeke and Randall J. Pederson, *Meet the Puritans: With a Guide to Modern Reprints* (Grand Rapids: Reformation Heritage Books, 2006), 584.

10. Robert Traill, *Justification Vindicated* (1692; repr., Edinburgh: Banner of Truth, 2002), 25–31.

instrumentality of faith alone. Far from being an isolated and negotiable doctrine, Traill viewed *sola fide* as integral to evangelical Christianity. "All the great fundamentals of Christian truth centre in this of justification," he wrote, and then added:

> The Trinity of Persons in the Godhead; the incarnation of the only begotten of the Father; the satisfaction paid to the law and justice of God for the sins of the world by his obedience and sacrifice of himself in that flesh he assumed; and the divine authority of the Scriptures which reveal all this; [these] are all straight lines of truth that centre in this doctrine of [the] justification of a sinner by the imputation and application of that satisfaction. [There can be] no justification without a righteousness; no righteousness can be but that which answers fully and perfectly the holy law of God; no such righteousness can be performed but by a divine person; no benefit can accrue to a sinner by it unless it be some way his and applied to him; no application can be made of this but by faith in Jesus Christ. And as the connection with and dependence of this truth upon the other great mysteries of divine truth is evident in the plain proposal of it, so the same has been sadly manifest in this, that the forsaking of the doctrine of justification by faith in Christ's righteousness has been the first step of apostasy in many, who have not stopped till they have revolted from Christianity itself.[11]

To pull on this thread is to unravel the whole scheme of the gospel. Christ's righteousness and human merit are antithetical. We are either saved by grace alone, or we are not saved at all.

> Law and gospel, faith and works, Christ's righteousness and our own, grace and debt, do equally divide all in this matter. Crafty men may endeavour to blend and mix these things together in justification, but it is a vain attempt. It is not only most expressly rejected in the gospel…but the nature of the things in themselves, and the sense and conscience of every

---

11. Traill, *Justification Vindicated*, 67.

serious person, do witness to the same, that our own righteousness, and Christ's righteousness, do comprehend all the pleas of men to justification—one or other of them every man in the world stands upon—and that they are inconsistent with, and destructive of, one another in justification. If a man trusts to his own righteousness, he rejects Christ's; if he trusts to Christ's righteousness, he rejects his own. If he will not reject his own righteousness, as too good to be renounced; if he will not venture on Christ's righteousness, as not sufficient alone to bear him out, and bring him safe off at God's bar, he is in both a convicted unbeliever. And if he endeavours to patch up a righteousness before God made up of both, he is still under the law, and a despiser of gospel grace (Gal. 2:21).[12]

2. Grace Alone through Christ Alone. The Puritans also emphasized how grace comes to us in and through Jesus Christ. Consider, for example, the six sermons on John 1:16 ("And of his fulness have all we received, and grace for grace") by William Bridge titled "Grace for Grace, or the Overflowings of Christ's Fulness Received by All Saints."[13] Bridge preached that "There is an infinite treasury of grace and holiness in Jesus Christ. This he hath not received for himself, but for others. There is an infinite propension [propensity] and willingness in him to give out this grace unto the children of men. And nothing either in heaven or earth can hinder him: surely therefore, there is the communication of fulness of Jesus Christ unto all believers."[14]

In his third sermon, Bridge said, "Whatsoever grace or holiness the saints and people of God have from Christ; they have it all in a way of receiving."[15] Bridge demonstrated this in relation to our justification, adoption, and sanctification and then offered five

---

12. Traill, *Justification Vindicated*, 69–70.
13. Bridge, *Grace for Grace*, in *Works*, 1:183–293.
14. Bridge, *Grace for Grace*, in *Works*, 1:211.
15. Bridge, *Grace for Grace*, in *Works*, 1:223.

arguments for why grace can only be had "in a way of receiving," namely: "the insufficiency of nature, the supernaturality of grace, the shortness of all means that are appointed thereunto, the work and nature of faith, and the posture and true behavior of prayer."[16]

Why does God choose to dispense his grace in this way? Bridge gave three reasons: (1) To take away all boasting, (2) To honor and exalt Jesus Christ, and (3) That the saints and children of God may live by faith.[17]

The Freedom God's Grace Brings

The Puritans exulted not only in the freedom of God's grace but also in the freedom that God's grace brings into the lives of believers. Grace is given freely, and freely given grace ushers us into a new state of liberty and freedom.

A particularly helpful book in this regard is *The True Bounds of Christian Freedom* by Samuel Bolton (1606–1654). Bolton wrote to both defend Christian liberty and to uphold the authority of God's law and the necessity of obedience in the Christian life. In his dedication, Bolton described his book like this: "It contains chiefly some friendly discussion of some opinions which have been maintained against the law of God, and in it I have endeavoured to uphold the law so as to show that it does not take away from the liberties of grace, and to establish grace so that the law is not made void, and so that believers are not set free from any duty they owe to God or man."[18]

Bolton's book is a closely reasoned, carefully nuanced look at gospel, law, and freedom, organized around six questions:

1. Whether our being made free by Christ frees us from the law.

---

16. Bridge, *Grace for Grace,* in *Works,* 1:225.
17. Bridge, *Grace for Grace,* in *Works,* 1:236–37.
18. Robert Bolton, *The True Bounds of Christian Freedom* (Edinburgh: Banner of Truth, 1978), 9–10.

2. Whether our being made free by Christ delivers us from all punishments or chastisements for sin.

3. Whether it is consistent with Christian freedom to be under obligation to perform duties because God has commanded them.

4. Whether Christ's freemen may come into bondage again through sin.

5. Whether it is consistent with Christian freedom to perform duties out of respect for the recompense of the reward.

6. Whether the freedom of a Christian frees him from all obedience to men.[19]

Bolton begins by asserting "that there is a true and real freedom which Christ has purchased, and into which He has brought all those who are true believers."[20] This freedom, he contends, is real, universal, and constant. It is a new state, into which the believer has been placed, having been delivered from his previous bondage to Satan, sin, and the law. "Wherever the Lord's jubilee is proclaimed and pronounced in a man's soul," Bolton writes, "he will never hear again of a return to bondage."[21] He then breaks down Christian freedom into two branches: "freedom in its negative aspects" and "freedom in its positive aspects."[22]

Bolton is especially helpful in explaining what it means to be freed from the law. Citing several Pauline texts, including Romans 6:14, "ye are not under the law, but under grace," Bolton shows that believers are free not only from the ceremonial law but also from the law as a covenant, and from the curses, accusations, and rigors of the law. "What a privilege is this, to be free from the curses and penalties of the law, so that if the law threatens, Christ promises; if the law curses, Christ blesses. This is a high privilege. If God

---

19. Bolton, *True Bounds of Christian Freedom*, 14.
20. Bolton, *True Bounds of Christian Freedom*, 19.
21. Bolton, *True Bounds of Christian Freedom*, 21.
22. Bolton, *True Bounds of Christian Freedom*, 22–50.

did but let one spark of His wrath and displeasure fall upon your conscience for sin, you would then know what a mercy it is to be thus freed."[23]

Bolton also outlines the positive aspects of Christian liberty, showing how we are freed not only *from* negative consequences but also *to* positive privileges. He lists seven:

1. We are freed from a state of wrath and bondage to a state of mercy and favour.

2. We are freed from a state of condemnation and brought to a state of justification.

3. We are freed from a state of enmity and brought into a state of friendship.

4. We are freed from a state of death and brought into a state of life.

5. We are freed from a state of sin and brought into a state of service.

6. We are freed from a state of bondage, a spirit of slavery in service, and brought into a spirit of sonship and liberty in service.

7. We are freed from death and hell and brought to life and glory.[24]

This sets the stage for Bolton's first query: "Are Christians freed from the moral law as a rule of obedience?"[25] Bolton is careful in his answer, acknowledging that there are texts "that seem to speak of the abrogation of the law,"[26] as well as "some Scriptures which seem to hold up the law, and which say that the law is still in force."[27] Then Bolton surveys the various meanings of

23. Bolton, *True Bounds of Christian Freedom,* 34.
24. Bolton, *True Bounds of Christian Freedom,* 48–49.
25. Bolton, *True Bounds of Christian Freedom,* 51.
26. Bolton, *True Bounds of Christian Freedom,* 52.
27. Bolton, *True Bounds of Christian Freedom,* 53.

the word "law" in Scripture, covering no less than seven different senses of the word. Only then does he get to the heart of the
issue: "Are believers freed from obedience to the moral law, that is,
from the moral law as a rule of obedience?"[28] Bolton here defines
the substance of the law as "the sum of doctrine concerning piety
towards God, charity towards our neighbours, [and] temperance
and sobriety towards ourselves."[29] He did not wish to quarrel with
those who say "we are freed from law, as given by Moses, and are
only tied to the obedience of it, as it is given in Christ,"[30] provided
there is agreement as to the fundamental authority of the law in
the lives of believers. "Acknowledge the moral law as a rule of obedience and Christian walking, and there will be no falling out,
whether you take it as promulgated by Moses, or as handed to you
and renewed by Christ."[31]

Bolton answers his first query with two propositions: "(1) That
the law, for the substance of it (for we speak not of the circumstances and accessories of it), remains as a rule of walking to the
people of God. (2) That there was no end or use for which the law
was originally given but is consistent with grace, and serviceable
to the advancement of the covenant grace."[32] Bolton then devotes
fifty pages to an exceptionally clear explanation and persuasive
defense of these propositions. In doing so, he both upholds the
freedom of God's grace and the freedom that God's grace brings
into our lives.

The Power of God's Grace

God's grace sets us free from Satan, sin, and the law because it
brings us under Christ's powerful and gracious reign. "For sin
shall not have dominion over you: for ye are not under the law,

---

28. Bolton, *True Bounds of Christian Freedom,* 57.
29. Bolton, *True Bounds of Christian Freedom,* 57.
30. Bolton, *True Bounds of Christian Freedom,* 57.
31. Bolton, *True Bounds of Christian Freedom,* 57.
32. Bolton, *True Bounds of Christian Freedom,* 59.

but under grace" (Rom. 6:14). The Puritans uniformly insisted that the grace that justifies also sanctifies. Grace is not only given to us freely: it also liberates us from slavery to sin. Far from being a license to sin, grace is God's effective deliverance from sin's dominion.

A helpful exposition of Romans 6:14 is found in John Owen's book *A Treatise of the Dominion of Sin and Grace*.[33] Owen distinguished between the respective dominions of sin and grace, reminding his readers that "Our souls are, and must be, under the rule of some principle or law.... We are either 'servants of sin unto death, or of obedience unto righteousness' (Rom. 6:16)."[34]

Following Paul's logic from Romans 6, Owen shows that "the state of the soul, as unto life and death eternal, follows the conduct and rule that we are under. If sin have the dominion, we are lost for ever; if it be dethroned, we are safe."[35] To say that sin is "dethroned" is not to deny the ongoing struggles with sin that believers experience. Sin "may tempt, seduce, and entice; it may fight, war, perplex, and disquiet; it may surprise into actual sin," Owen writes; "yet if it have not the dominion in us, we are in a state of grace and acceptation with God."[36] The great promise given to believers in Romans 6:14 is that "though [sin] will abide in us, though it will contend for rule by deceit and force, yet it shall not prevail, it shall not have the dominion."[37]

Owen organized his treatise around three inquiries:

1. What is that dominion of sin which we are freed from and discharged of by grace?

---

33. John Owen, *A Treatise of the Dominion of Sin and Grace*, in *The Works of John Owen*, ed. W. H. Goold (1850–1853; repr., Edinburgh: Banner of Truth, 1996), 7:499–560. A modernization of this book is scheduled to be published in Reformation Heritage Books' Puritan Treasures for Today series.

34. Owen, *Dominion of Sin and Grace*, in *Works*, 7:508.

35. Owen, *Dominion of Sin and Grace*, in *Works*, 7:508.

36. Owen, *Dominion of Sin and Grace*, in *Works*, 7:508.

37. Owen, *Dominion of Sin and Grace*, in *Works*, 7:508.

2. How may we know whether sin hath the dominion in us or not?

3. What is the reason and grounds of the assurance here given us that sin shall not have dominion over us;—namely, because we are "not under the law, but under grace"?[38]

In the course of his work, Owen expounds the liberating power of God's grace in the life of the believer with exegetical care and experiential application, highlighting the nature and signs of sin's dominion and the overthrow of this dominion by God's triumphant grace.

1. The Nature of Sin's Dominion. In answer to his first inquiry, Owen delineates several characteristic features of sin's dominion. First, it is "usurped" because "sin hath no right to rule in the souls of men."[39] Sin's reign is "evil and perverse, not only because it is unjust and usurped" but also because it always leads to the "hurt and ruin" of its subjects.[40] Second, "this dominion of sin is not a mere force against the will and endeavours of them that are under it."[41] Strong temptations to sin do not constitute the dominion of sin. In fact, sin may perplex people with its temptations while not bearing rule over them. Where sin does have dominion, "it hath the force and power of a law in the wills and minds of them in whom it is."[42] That's why Paul describes people in terms of willing slaves who yield obedience to sin's ruling power (see Rom. 6:16). This means that for sin to have dominion, "there is required a consent of the will in some measure and degree…. If the will of sinning be taken away, sin cannot have dominion."[43] Third, the dominion of sin is exclusive of all other lords. Owen shows that

---

38. Owen, *Dominion of Sin and Grace*, in *Works*, 7:508.
39. Owen, *Dominion of Sin and Grace*, in *Works*, 7:509.
40. Owen, *Dominion of Sin and Grace*, in *Works*, 7:512.
41. Owen, *Dominion of Sin and Grace*, in *Works*, 7:512.
42. Owen, *Dominion of Sin and Grace*, in *Works*, 7:512.
43. Owen, *Dominion of Sin and Grace*, in *Works*, 7:512–13.

"grace and sin may be in the same soul at the same time, but they cannot bear rule in the same soul at the same time."[44] There is only one throne in the human heart, and it will seat only one ruler. To be under the reign of grace is to be free from sin's tyranny. The fourth feature of sin's dominion is that it "makes the soul sensible of its power and rule," unless, as Owen clarifies, the conscience becomes "utterly seared and hardened, and so 'past feeling.'"[45] Sin will do this in two ways: by suppressing conviction in the mind and by constantly soliciting the mind and affections with temptations to sin.

2. The Signs of Sin's Dominion. Owen begins his second inquiry, "How may we know whether sin hath the dominion in us or not[?]" by stating the practical and pastoral concern behind his treatise. "An inquiry this is which is very necessary for some to make, and for all to have rightly determined in their minds, from Scripture and experience; for on that determination depends all our solid peace. Sin will be in us; it will lust, fight, and entice us;— but *the great question*, as unto our peace and comfort, is, whether it hath dominion over us or no."[46]

Owen's answer to this great question is very carefully nuanced and will provoke thorough self-examination in thoughtful readers. There are clear lines drawn. For those who "openly wear sin's livery,"[47] the reign of sin is obvious. Owen is not here trying to discern whether openly rebellious and wicked people are Christians: such are clearly the avowed servants of sin—regardless of their religious profession or affiliation.

But for others, the case is more difficult to determine, for, "on the one hand, they may have sundry things in them which may seem repugnant unto the reign of sin" but actually are not.

---

44. Owen, *Dominion of Sin and Grace,* in *Works,* 7:513.
45. Owen, *Dominion of Sin and Grace,* in *Works,* 7:515.
46. Owen, *Dominion of Sin and Grace,* in *Works,* 7:518.
47. Owen, *Dominion of Sin and Grace,* in *Works,* 7:518.

It is quite possible for people to remain in sin's slavery, in spite of religious knowledge, changed affections, outward duties, partial repentance, and resolves against committing future sins. "No man," contends Owen, "can be acquitted by pleas taken from [these things] as unto his subjection to the reign of sin."[48]

On the other hand, there are arguments that "may be taken to prove the dominion of sin in any person, which yet will not certainly do it."[49] Here, Owen covers a number of dangerous symptoms, which should certainly cause concern and prompt self-examination but which do not necessarily mean that someone is under sin's sway. These pages contain some of the most penctrating, soul-searching spiritual analyses in Owen's writings and invite careful and prayerful meditation.

Owen then lists ten incontrovertible signs of sin's dominion, which, he says, "need neither proof nor illustration":

1. It is so where sin hath possessed the will. And it hath possessed the will when there are no restraints from sinning taken from its nature, but from its consequents only.

2. When men proclaim their sins and hide them not,—when they boast in them and of them, as it is with multitudes; or,

3. Approve of themselves in any known sin, without renewed repentance, as drunkenness, uncleanness, swearing, and the like; or,

4. Live in the neglect of religious duties in their closets and families, whence all their public attendance unto them is but hypocrisy; or,

5. Have an enmity to true holiness and the power of godliness; or,

6. Are visible apostates from profession, especially if they add, as is usual, persecution to their apostasy; or,

---

48. Owen, *Dominion of Sin and Grace,* in *Works,* 7:519.
49. Owen, *Dominion of Sin and Grace,* in *Works,* 7:519.

7. Are ignorant of the sanctifying principles of the gospel and Christian religion; or,

8. Are despisers of the means of conversion; or,

9. Live in security under open providential warnings and calls to repentance; or,

10. Are enemies in their minds unto the true interest of Christ in the world.[50]

Where these things and the like are found, there is no question what it is that hath dominion and bears rule in the minds of men.[51]

3. The Overthrow of Sin's Dominion through Grace.

This leads to Owen's third inquiry concerning the grounds and assurance that sin shall not have dominion over believers. This is where Owen drills into the promise of Romans 6:14, that we "are not under the law, but under grace."

Owen shows that sin's dominion can be overthrown only by another and stronger force or power, and that this power is not from the law: "Sin will neither be cast nor kept out of its throne, but by a spiritual power and strength in the soul to oppose, conquer, and dethrone it. Where it is not conquered it will reign; and conquered it will not be without a mighty prevailing power: this the law will not, cannot give."[52]

In fact, "the law gives no liberty of any kind," but rather leads to "bondage, and so cannot free us from any dominion...but this

---

50. Owen, *Dominion of Sin and Grace*, in *Works*, 7:541.

51. Owen, *Dominion of Sin and Grace*, in *Works*, 7:541–42.

52. Owen, *Dominion of Sin and Grace*, in *Works*, 7:542. It should be said that Owen shows that the law can be taken in two different ways: "1. For the whole revelation of the mind and will of God in the Old Testament" and "2. For the covenantal rule of perfect obedience: 'Do this and live.'" (7:542–43). When Paul says that we are "not under the law," Owen understands law in this second sense: thus, it is the law in this covenantal sense that cannot secure liberty from sin. In no way does Owen deny the normative use of the law in establishing the standard for righteousness and holiness.

we have also by the gospel."[53] Nor does the law "supply us with effectual motives and encouragements to endeavour the ruin of the dominion of sin in a way of duty."[54] Owen goes even further, declaring that "Christ is not in the law; he is not proposed in it, not communicated by it,—we are not made partakers of him thereby."[55] This we find only in the grace of the gospel. "In it is Christ revealed; by it he is proposed and exhibited unto us; thereby we are made partakers of him and all the benefits of his mediation."[56]

In his final chapter, Owen discloses how God's grace overthrows sin and secures liberty and freedom for believers. Readers should especially note three things:

1. The meritorious procuring cause of this liberty is the death and blood of Jesus Christ.

2. The internal efficient cause of this liberty, or that whereby the power and rule of sin is destroyed in us, is the Holy Spirit himself.

3. The instrumental cause of this freedom is the duty of believers themselves in and for the destruction of sin.[57]

In those three statements, Owen provides the essential coordinates from which he maps a full theology of sanctification and holiness in other places, especially in his treatise *Of the Mortification of Sin in Believers*[58] and Book 4 in *Pneumatologia: A Discourse Concerning the Holy Spirit.*[59] He thus joins doctrine and duty, truth and practice, showing us how God's sanctifying grace comes to us through the cross of Christ and the ministry of the Spirit, while

---

53. Owen, *Dominion of Sin and Grace*, in *Works*, 7:549.
54. Owen, *Dominion of Sin and Grace*, in *Works*, 7:550.
55. Owen, *Dominion of Sin and Grace*, in *Works*, 7:551.
56. Owen, *Dominion of Sin and Grace*, in *Works*, 7:551.
57. Owen, *Dominion of Sin and Grace*, in *Works*, 7:553–54.
58. Owen, *Of the Mortification of Sin in Believers*, in *Works*, 6:1–86.
59. Owen, Book 4 of *Pneumatologia: A Discourse Concerning the Holy Spirit*, in *Works*, 3:366–565. See also chapter 6 in this book.

also empowering us to live in practical obedience to God through faith in Christ and dependence on the Spirit. Owen would have agreed with the words of Charles Wesley's (1707–1788) great hymn, written fifty-one years later:

> He breaks the power of cancelled sin,
> He sets the prisoner free;
> His blood can make the foulest clean;
> His blood availed for me.[60]

Questions for Reflection and Discussion

1. In your own spiritual life, do you tend to drift more toward the "frozen north" with its "arctic dangers of icy legalism and frigid formalism," or the "swampy south" and its "tropical dangers of sultry self-indulgence and lazy licentiousness"?

2. In your own words, how would you explain the difference between the freedom *of* God's grace in our justification and the freedom God's grace brings *into* our lives in sanctification? Why should justification and sanctification always be distinguished but never be separated?

3. As you examine your life, do you see troubling evidences of the dominion of sin? If so, do not delay in turning to Christ in repentance and faith.

---

60. Charles Wesley, "O For a Thousand Tongues to Sing," 1739.

6

THE PURITANS
Engage Our Wills in the Pursuit of Practical Holiness

This whole matter of sanctification and holiness is peculiarly joined with and limited unto the doctrine, truth, and grace of the gospel, for holiness is nothing but the implanting, writing, and realizing of the gospel in our souls.

—JOHN OWEN[1]

"Holiness is a most beautiful and lovely thing. We drink in strange notions of holiness from our childhood, as if it were a melancholy, morose, sour and unpleasant thing; but there is nothing in it but what is sweet and ravishingly lovely."[2] So wrote Jonathan Edwards, the eighteenth-century New England Puritan, in his *Miscellanies*.

Edwards's observation captures well the conflicting thoughts and feelings people have about sanctification and holiness. Some people associate holiness with all that is sour and dour in religion. When others hear the word "holy," they immediately think of the self-righteous "holier-than-thou" attitude that looks and sounds more like Pharisaism than likeness to Christ.

---

1. John Owen, *Pneumatologia: A Discourse Concerning the Holy Spirit,* in *The Works of John Owen* (1850–1853; repr., Edinburgh: Banner of Truth, 1965–1968), 3:370–71.

2. Jonathan Edwards, *The Miscellanies: a–500,* Thomas A. Schafer, ed., *The Works of Jonathan Edwards* (New Haven, Conn.: Yale University Press, 1994), 13:163.

But Edwards is right. In spite of these "strange notions" that harbor in our hearts, genuine holiness is "sweet and ravishingly lovely." In the words of Thomas Brooks (1608–1680), "Holiness differs nothing from happiness but in name. Holiness is happiness in the bud, and happiness is holiness at the full. Happiness is nothing but the quintessence of holiness."[3] If that quote doesn't put to rest the idea that Puritanism is "the haunting fear that someone, somewhere, may be happy,"[4] I don't know what will!

The Puritans have much to teach us about holiness, including its necessity, nature, source, pattern, and means.

The Necessity of Holiness

The absolute necessity of holiness is a common theme in Puritan writings. They believed that sanctification is the necessary fruit of justification and an essential prerequisite to enjoying the beatific vision in heaven. They often quoted Hebrews 12:14: "Follow peace with all men, and holiness, without which no man shall see the Lord." In his treatise on this text, Brooks stated his doctrine like this: "that real holiness is the only way to happiness. All men must be holy on earth, or they shall never see the beatifical vision, they shall never reach to a glorious fruition of God in heaven."[5] Owen agreed: "There is no imagination wherewith mankind is besotted more foolish, none so pernicious, as this, that persons not purified, not sanctified, not made holy, in this life, should afterward be taken into that state of blessedness which consists in the enjoyment of God."[6]

---

3. Thomas Brooks, *The Crown and Glory of Christianity,* or *Holiness the Only Way to Happiness,* in Alexander B. Grosart, ed., *The Works of Thomas Brooks* (Edinburgh: Banner of Truth, 2002), 4:37.

4. H. L. Mencken, *A Mencken Chrestomathy* (New York: Vintage Books, 1982), 624.

5. Brooks, *Crown and Glory of Christianity,* in *Works,* 4:37.

6. Owen, *Pneumatologia,* in *Works,* 3:574.

The Puritans not only urged the necessity of sanctification but also grounded the need for holiness in the truth of the gospel, "the doctrine which is according to godliness" (1 Tim. 6:3, cf. Titus 1:1). Against antinomians, they emphasized the necessity of practical holiness and obedience to God's moral law. Against Socinians and Papists (Roman Catholics), they believed that holiness is the fruit of the Reformed and evangelical doctrines of God's sovereign electing grace, Christ's substitutionary atonement, justification through the imputation of Christ's righteousness through the instrumentality of faith alone, the effectual work of the Spirit in regeneration and conversion, and the preservation and perseverance of the saints.[7] In Owen's words, "the Scripture doth so place the foundations of all true and real holiness in these things, that without the faith of them, and an influence on our minds from them, it will not allow any thing to be so called."[8] Owen thus devoted Book 5 of *Pneumatologia: A Discourse Concerning the Holy Spirit*, to the necessity of holiness. He argued for the need for holiness from five distinct angles: (1) the nature of God, (2) eternal election, (3) the commands of God, (4) the work of Christ, and (5) our condition in this world.

The church today is adrift in a sea of antinomianism. The hollowing out of twentieth-century evangelicalism, the widespread influence of hyper-dispensationalist "free grace" theology, and the insurgence of progressive post-evangelical views of Scripture have left many professing Christians without any moorings to the biblical injunction, "Be holy for I am holy, says the LORD" (see Lev. 11:44–45, 19:2, 20:7, 26, 21:8; Deut. 23:14; 1 Peter 1:15–16). In this void, the Puritans speak with biblical authority, practical clarity, and persuasive urgency. "Our principle duty in this world," said Owen, "is, to know aright, what it is to be holy, and to be so indeed."[9] That leads us to the next consideration:

---

7. See especially Owen, *Pneumatologia*, in *Works*, 3:566–651.
8. Owen, *Pneumatologia*, in *Works*, 3:567.
9. Owen, *Pneumatologia*, in *Works*, 3:370.

The Nature of Holiness

The Puritans, following Calvin and the Reformers, drew a careful distinction between justification and sanctification. While justification concerns the forensic (legal) aspect of salvation, sanctification addresses the ethical (moral). Justification addresses the guilt and penalty of sin and changes our legal status before the divine Judge from "guilty" to "righteous." Sanctification, on the other hand, tackles the power and pollution of sin, rendering us definitively free from sin's dominion while progressively purifying us from sin's defilement and renewing us in the image of God. There are, then, both definitive and progressive aspects to sanctification, each of which includes both negative and positive dimensions.

The Puritans cover the full spectrum of the doctrine of sanctification, though not always in one place. For example, many of their books are narrowly focused on a single aspect of the progressive/negative dimension, such as mortification, repentance, or even one specific sin. Consider for example, Thomas Watson's *Doctrine of Repentance* and John Owen's trilogy of books on mortification, temptation, and indwelling sin, now published together as *Overcoming Sin and Temptation*.[10]

Other books emphasize one or more of the positive aspects of piety and godliness. These include books on specific "graces" or virtues, such as faith, love, or contentment, like Jeremiah Burroughs's *Rare Jewel of Christian Contentment,* as well as manuals on the "means" for cultivating godliness or walking with God. Examples of these include *Holy Helps for a Godly Life* by Richard Rogers (1551–1618), *The Practice of Piety* by Lewis Bayly (c. 1575–1631), and *The Christian's Daily Walk* by Henry Scudder (c. 1585–1652). In addition to these, we can add the many examples of Puritan casuistry, books that were essentially counseling manuals written to address a wide variety of case studies.[11] One of the most helpful

---

10. John Owen, *Overcoming Sin and Temptation*, ed. Kelly M. Kapic and Justin Taylor (Wheaton, Ill.: Crossway, 2015).

11. For more information, see "Puritan Casuistry: An Interview with Tim

and encouraging of these is *A Lifting Up for the Downcast,* a biblical and pastoral treatment of depression, by William Bridge.[12] Two other recently republished examples are John Flavel's *The Cure for Sinful Fear* and *The Cure for Unjust Anger* by John Downame (1571–1652).

But Puritan authors also produced thorough treatises on holiness that aimed to connect the dots between justification and sanctification, law and grace, and faith and practice. One of the best examples, and a book to which we'll return below, is *The Gospel Mystery of Sanctification* by Walter Marshall (1628–1680). When reading the Puritans, it is important to consider the intention and scope of any given work.

Broadly considered, the Puritans defined holiness in terms of: (1) the purification of our natures from the defilement and pollution of sin; (2) the renovation of the whole man (spirit, soul, and body) according to the image of God; (3) conformity to God's holy character, as expressed in his moral law and exemplified in the holy humanity of the Lord Jesus Christ; and (4) personal obedience to God in the power of the Holy Spirit, expressed in practical piety in every sphere of life, including personal life (thoughts, affections, desires, habits, and words), life in the home (with a strong emphasis on the relative duties of husbands, wives, parents, and children), and public life (in relation to both the church and the state).

John Owen, who is often noted for his comprehensive approach to almost every topic he considered, provided a thorough analysis of the nature of holiness in Book 4 of *Pneumatologia.* His definition combines the warp of biblical-theological categories (doctrines of God, Christ, the Spirit, and covenants) with the woof of practical

---

Challies by Joel Beeke," https://banneroftruth.org/us/resources/articles/2014/puritan-casuistry/. Accessed October 31, 2019, and "Puritan Casuistry," in Joel R. Beeke and Mark Jones, *A Puritan Theology: Doctrine for Life* (Grand Rapids: Reformation Heritage Books, 2012), 927–45.

12. For more discussion of Owen on temptation, Burroughs on contentment, and Bridge on depression, see chapter 10.

and pastoral theology (cleansing from sin, spiritual renewal, and obedience to God): "Sanctification is an immediate work of the Spirit of God on the souls of believers, purifying and cleansing of their natures from the pollution and uncleanness of sin, renewing in them the image of God, and thereby enabling them, from a spiritual and habitual principle of grace, to yield obedience unto God, according unto the tenor and terms of the new covenant, by virtue of the life and death of Jesus Christ."[13]

Owen's definition of sanctification not only weaves together the various threads of purification, renovation, conformity, and obedience but also anticipates our next consideration, the source of holiness.

The Source of Holiness

God's saving grace, revealed in the Lord Jesus Christ, declared in the gospel, applied by the Holy Spirit, and received by faith, is the fountain from which all the streams of holiness flow. The Puritans could emphasize different aspects of God's gracious work in sanctification, depending on the context and focus of their particular sermons or discourses, but all would have agreed with the Shorter Catechism that "sanctification is the work of God's free grace."[14]

Owen gave special attention to the role of the gospel in our sanctification. "This whole matter of sanctification and holiness is peculiarly joined with and limited unto the *doctrine, truth*, and *grace* of the gospel," he wrote, "for holiness is nothing but the implanting, writing, and realizing of the gospel in our souls."[15] This accounts for his common use of "gospel" as an adjective—as in "gospel holiness."[16] "Gospel truth is the only root whereon gospel

13. Owen, *Pneumatologia,* in *Works,* 3:386.
14. Westminster Shorter Catechism, Q. 35.
15. Owen, *Pneumatologia,* in *Works,* 3:370–71.
16. See, for example, John Owen, *The Nature of Apostasy from the Profession of the Gospel and the Punishment of Apostates Declared,* in *Works,* 7:162, 164, 166, 168, 170, 173–175, 177, 179, 181–182, 188, 192, 201, 226, 237, 239, 250, 256, 258.

holiness will grow."[17] "Gospel holiness," for Owen, was a shorthand description for an evangelical approach to sanctification, rooted in a full-orbed covenantal scheme of grace that embraces God's gracious electing purpose, Christ's finished work as our Mediator, and the efficacious grace of God's Spirit, who regenerates, indwells, and sanctifies all who are redeemed. In *Pneumatologia*, Owen zooms in on the particular work of the Holy Spirit in our sanctification: "It is the Holy Ghost who is the immediate peculiar sanctifier of all believers, and the author of all holiness in them."[18]

One of the most important Puritan books on sanctification arose from the personal doubts and struggles of Walter Marshall, who experienced years of spiritual conflict in his quest for holiness and assurance. Marshall read many of Richard Baxter's practical treatises on holy living but did not find them helpful. He finally found help after confessing his sins and struggles to Thomas Goodwin, his senior by twenty-eight years. After hearing Marshall's confession, Goodwin pointed out that he had forgotten to confess the greatest of all sins—unbelief. Under Goodwin's direction, Marshall began to focus on the person and work of Christ. This changed the course of his life and ministry, leading him to deeper holiness and true peace of conscience.

Out of this experience, Marshall wrote *The Gospel Mystery of Sanctification,* which was published twelve years after his death, and which Professor John Murray (1898–1975) called "the most important book on sanctification ever written."[19] At the heart of Marshall's book is the doctrine of the believer's union with Christ. In fourteen "directions," Marshall argued that gospel sanctification flows from faith in the finished work of Jesus Christ and fellowship with Him through the power of the Spirit. Though holiness

17. Owen, *The Nature of Apostasy,* in *Works,* 7:188.
18. Owen, *Pneumatologia,* in *Works,* 3:385.
19. Bruce H. McRae, "Introduction," in Walter Marshall, *The Gospel Mystery of Sanctification, A New Version, Put into English* (Eugene, Ore.: Wipf & Stock Publishers, 2005), 5.

is to be pursued and all the means of grace used to that end, the wellspring of all holy living is Christ's inexhaustible fullness.

> One great mystery is that the holy frame and disposition, by which our souls are furnished and enabled for immediate practice of the law, must be obtained by receiving it out of Christ's fullness, as a thing already prepared and brought to an existence for us in Christ and treasured up in Him; and that as we are justified by a righteousness wrought out in Christ and imputed to us, so we are sanctified by such a holy frame and qualifications as are first wrought out and completed in Christ for us, and then imparted to us…. This mystery is so great that notwithstanding all the light of the gospel, we commonly think that we must get a holy frame by producing it anew in ourselves and by forming and working it out of our own hearts. Therefore many that are seriously devout take a great deal of pains to mortify their corrupt nature and beget a holy frame of heart in themselves by striving earnestly to master their sinful lusts, and by pressing vehemently on their hearts many motives to godliness, laboring importunately to squeeze good qualifications out of them, as oil out of a flint. They account that, though they may be justified by a righteousness wrought out by Christ, yet they must be sanctified by a holiness wrought out of themselves.[20]

It seems that Marshall had in his crosshairs the same kind of legalistic striving for holiness that had characterized his own life. The problem with such striving is that it does not flow from the "holy frame" of a regenerate heart. As Marshall states in Direction V, "We cannot attain to the Practice of true holiness, by any of our endeavours, while we continue in our natural state, and are not partakers of a new state, by union and fellowship with Christ through faith."[21]

---

20. Walter Marshall, *The Gospel Mystery of Sanctification* (Grand Rapids: Reformation Heritage Books, 1999), 27–28.
21. Marshall, *The Gospel Mystery of Sanctification,* 53.

This doesn't mean, however, that there is no place for using the means of grace, such as self-examination, meditation, and prayer. Marshall encourages the use of all these means under Direction XIII. But Marshall was concerned that many people did not know how to use the means correctly: "The right use of the means of grace, is a point wherein many are ignorant, that use them with great zeal and diligence; and thereby they not only lose their labour, and the benefit of the means, but also they wrest and pervert them to their own destruction."[22]

This explains why Marshall began his approach to sanctification with first principles and laid the foundation for holy living in the mystery of the believer's union with Christ, from whose fullness we derive "all things that pertain unto life and godliness" (2 Peter 1:3) and "in whom are hid all the treasures of wisdom and knowledge" (Col. 2:3). The first step in living a holy life is not our work, but Christ's. This is why Marshall insists that "we are not at all to work together with Christ, in making or producing that holy frame in us, but only to take it to ourselves, and use it in our holy practice, as ready made to our hands. Thus we have fellowship with Christ in receiving that holy frame of spirit that was originally in him."[23]

There is, in other words, an order to the Christian life. Grace comes before works. Justification is first, while sanctification follows. Faith precedes the fruits of faith. As Marshall states in Direction VIII, "Be sure to seek for holiness of heart and life only in its due order, where God hath placed it, after union with Christ, justification, and the gift of the Holy Ghost; and, in that order, seek it earnestly by faith, as a very necessary part of your salvation."[24]

---

22. Marshall, *The Gospel Mystery of Sanctification*, 186.
23. Marshall, *The Gospel Mystery of Sanctification*, 28.
24. Marshall, *The Gospel Mystery of Sanctification*, 96.

The Pattern of Holiness

The believer's union with Jesus Christ in His death and resurrection provides the basic template or pattern for practical holiness. This pattern, grounded in Romans 6:5–9, is evident in the Westminster Shorter Catechism, question 35: "Sanctification is the work of God's free grace, whereby we are renewed in the whole man after the image of God, and are enabled more and more to die unto sin, and live unto righteousness." We see the same emphasis, with slightly different language, in Samuel Rutherford's Catechism: "Q. What are the parts of sanctification? A. In removing of the stony heart and slaying of sin, and a quickening of us to love righteousness (Ezek. 36:26–27)."[25] The practical appropriation of our union with Christ in his death and resurrection, through our own death to sin and living unto righteousness—or our mortification and vivification—is the pattern of gospel holiness.

John Owen, as many are aware, wrote the most widely read book on mortifying sin, in which he asked, "Do you mortify, do you make it your daily work; be always at it whilst you live; cease not a day from this work; be killing sin or it will be killing you."[26] Though Owen's treatise is short, comprising only eighty-six pages in volume 6 of his *Works*, it is a thorough, heart-probing, soul-searching book. But no one should think that Owen fell into the danger excoriated by Walter Marshall (see above), for Owen insisted that mortification is the proper work only of believers. "Unless a man be a believer,—that is, one that is truly ingrafted into Christ,—he can never mortify any one sin."[27]

Furthermore, Owen clarified that "we have all our mortification from the gift of Christ, and all the gifts of Christ are communicated to us and given us by the Spirit of Christ."[28] To

---

25. Samuel Rutherford, *Rutherford's Catechism: Containing the Sum of Christian Religion* (Edinburgh: Blue Banner Productions, 1998), 56.
26. Owen, *Of the Mortification of Sin in Believers*, in *Works*, 6:9.
27. Owen, *Of the Mortification of Sin*, in *Works*, 6:33.
28. Owen, *Of the Mortification of Sin*, in *Works*, 6:19.

attempt mortification apart from the Spirit is, therefore, the height of folly. "Mortification from a self-strength, carried on by ways of self-invention, unto the end of a self-righteousness, is the soul and substance of all false religion in the world."[29] How, then, does the Spirit empower believers to mortify sin? "He brings the cross of Christ into the heart of a sinner by faith, and gives us communion with Christ in his death, and fellowship in his sufferings."[30] Therefore, Owen exhorts,

> Set faith at work on Christ for the killing of thy sin. His blood is the great sovereign remedy for sin-sick souls. Live in this, and thou wilt die a conqueror; yea, thou wilt, through the good providence of God, live to see thy lust dead at thy feet.... Act faith peculiarly upon the death, blood, and cross of Christ; that is, on Christ as crucified and slain. Mortification of sin is peculiarly from the death of Christ.... Let faith look on Christ in the gospel as he is set forth dying and crucified for us. Look on him under the weight of our sins, praying, bleeding, dying; bring him in that condition into thy heart by faith; apply his blood so shed to thy corruptions: do this daily.[31]

Along with mortification, another necessary part of practical holiness is vivification. Not only must we die to sin; we must live to righteousness. We are raised with Christ to walk in newness of life. Owen describes this as "the positive work of the Spirit in the sanctification of believers."[32] And, once again, he goes out of his way to ground all his practical exhortations to holiness on the foundation of the Spirit's effectual work in the hearts of believers. Consider, for example, the following two assertions, offered by Owen "in the declaration and vindication of gospel sanctification and holiness":

---

29. Owen, *Of the Mortification of Sin,* in *Works,* 6:7.
30. Owen, *Of the Mortification of Sin,* in *Works,* 6:19.
31. Owen, *Of the Mortification of Sin,* in *Works,* 6:79, 83, 85.
32. Owen, *Pneumatologia,* in *Works,* 3:468.

I. There is wrought and preserved in the minds and souls of all believers, by the Spirit of God, a supernatural principle or habit of grace and holiness, whereby they are made meet for and enabled to live unto God, and perform that obedience which he requireth and accepteth through Christ in the covenant of grace; essentially or specifically distinct from all natural habits, intellectual and moral, however or by what means soever acquired or improved.

II. There is an immediate work or effectual operation of the Holy Spirit by his grace required unto every act of holy obedience, whether internal only in faith and love, or external also; that is, unto all the holy actings of our understandings, wills, and affections, and unto all duties of obedience in our walking before God.[33]

With this foundation in place, Owen goes on to explain three duties required of us:

(1) We must "carefully and diligently...use all means to cherish and preserve it [the Spirit-wrought principle of holiness and spiritual life] in our hearts."

(2) We are to "manifest it by its fruits, in the mortification of corrupt lusts and affections, [and] in all duties of holiness, righteousness, charity, and piety, in the world."

(3) We must "be thankful for what we have received."[34]

The Means of Holiness

That leads us, finally, to the means of holiness.[35] As with all the constituent parts of the doctrine of sanctification, the Puritans wrote entire treatises on the means for cultivating godliness.

---

33. Owen, *Pneumatologia, in Works*, 3:472.
34. Owen, *Pneumatologia, in Works*, 3:482.
35. Portions of this section have been adapted from Brian G. Hedges's preface to Richard Rogers's book, *Holy Helps for a Godly Life* (Grand Rapids: Reformation Heritage Books, 2018), vii–xxiv.

One of the first was Richard Rogers, who devoted the third of his *Seven Treatises* to "the means, whereby a godly life is helped and continued."[36] As O. R. Johnston (1927–1985) observed, "Rogers' work is of paramount importance here, for he seems to have been the first man explicitly to state the nature and aims of meditation as a scriptural means of grace."[37] In fact, Rogers was the first Puritan to treat these means in a systematic and cohesive way. Though Calvin and the other Reformers had written much about prayer and the sacraments, and though general exhortations to devotional practices were scattered in the sermons and treatises of William Perkins (1558–1602) and Richard Greenham (1535–1594), Rogers was apparently the first Protestant to compile a full list of the means of grace, both public and private, to help Christians in the pursuit of godliness.

In his introductory remarks, Rogers explains: "The Christian life is upheld and continued by means. Everyone who sets upon this life will desire to know these means and how to rightly use them, because the hindrances and discouragements in the Christian life are many and great. It is therefore fitting for me to show what I understand by these means or helps.... As the Christian life does not begin without means, neither can it grow without them."[38]

In defining these means or helps, Rogers says, "The means God has appointed to help His people to continue and grow in a godly life, are those religious exercises, by which Christians may be made fit to practice it."[39] These he divides into ordinary and extraordinary and public and private. The public (and ordinary) means are the preaching of the Word, the sacraments, and public

---

36. Richard Rogers, *Seven Treatises* (London: Felix Kynston, for Thomas Man, 1616) from "The Sum of all the Seven Treatises, and the contents of every chapter in them," 35.

37. O. R. Johnston, "The Means of Grace in Puritan Theology," *The Evangelical Quarterly* 25, no. 4 (1953): 202–23.

38. Rogers, *Holy Helps for a Godly Life*, 1.

39. Rogers, *Holy Helps for a Godly Life*, 2.

prayers, with the singing of psalms. Rogers lists seven private (also ordinary) helps, namely: watchfulness, meditation, putting and keeping on the Christian armor, reflection on personal spiritual experience, godly conversation with other believers and within one's family, private prayer, and the reading of both Scripture and godly literature. Finally, Rogers addresses two extraordinary means: solemn thanksgiving and fasting.

According to William Haller (1885–1974), Rogers's work "was the first important exposition of the code of behavior which expressed the English Calvinist, or more broadly speaking, the Puritan conception of the spiritual and moral life. As such it inaugurated a literature the extent and influence of which... can hardly be exaggerated."[40]

Of the dozens of practical books on holiness that appeared over the next one hundred years, several titles stand out. One of the best is Thomas Watson's *Heaven Taken by Storm,* a book that emphasized "the holy violence a Christian is to put forth in the pursuit of glory."[41] Watson described how the Christian, in pursuing heaven, must exercise violence against himself, Satan, and the world, and he included full chapters on how to do this through reading the Word, hearing the Word, prayer, meditation, self-examination, sanctifying the Lord's Day, and holy conversation with other believers.

Another helpful book is *The Christian's Daily Walk in Holy Peace and Security* by Henry Scudder, which made a strong impression on John Owen as a young man. Scudder discusses the importance of walking with God and provides specific instructions for how to begin the day with God, walk with God throughout the day, walk

---

40. William Haller, *The Rise of Puritanism* (New York: Columbia University Press, 1938), 36.

41. Thomas Watson, *Heaven Taken by Storm: Showing the Holy Violence a Christian Is to Put Forth in the Pursuit After Glory* (Grand Rapids: Reformation Heritage Books, 1992).

with God when alone or in company with others, walk with God in adversity and prosperity, and more.

Just as the Puritans' emphasis on grace and union with Christ can protect believers from legalistic and self-righteous striving, so their emphasis on the means of cultivating holiness can steer us away from undue passivity in our Christian lives. There is no holiness apart from union with Christ and the power of His indwelling Spirit. But the Spirit works through means—particularly the means of the Word and prayer. The practical pursuit of holiness, then, must include both faithful dependence upon the Lord *and* active appropriation of, and obedience to, His Word in our lives. Owen puts it well: "The Holy Ghost works in us and upon us, as we are fit to be wrought in and upon; that is, so as to preserve our own liberty and free obedience. He works upon our understandings, wills, consciences, and affections, agreeably to their own natures; he works *in us* and *with us*, not *against* us or *without* us; so that his assistance is an encouragement as to the facilitating of the work, and no occasion of neglect as to the work itself."[42]

As we conclude this chapter, let me encourage you to take inventory of your own walk with God. Are you pursuing holiness? Are you living out the gospel pattern of Christ's death and resurrection? Are you exercising holy violence against your sins and yourself, the world, the flesh, and the devil? Have you learned how to use the means of godliness as helps for living a holy and godly life? Do you know how to walk with God? Most importantly, are you united to Christ through faith and the indwelling of the Holy Spirit? Wherever you are in your pilgrimage to the Celestial City, I hope you will consider allowing the Puritans to become your traveling companions, your comrades in the good fight of faith and the pursuit of personal, practical holiness.

---

42. Owen, *Of the Mortification of Sin*, in *Works*, 6:20.

Questions for Reflection and Discussion

1. What "strange notions" or misconceptions about holiness have shaped your thinking about this vital aspect of Christian living? How has this chapter enlarged, or even corrected, your perspective on holiness?

2. How is practical holiness connected to our union with Christ? Why is all striving for holiness apart from dependence on Christ and His Spirit doomed to failure?

3. On the other hand, how does the Puritan emphasis on "means" protect us from undue passivity in the pursuit of holiness? Are you both depending on Christ and faithfully using the means of grace?

7

THE PURITANS
Equip the Saints in the Battle against the World, the Flesh, and the Devil

In the spiritual conflict we need weapons not only defensive but offensive; not only the shield of faith, but the sword of the Spirit, that we may destroy and slay sin, and withstand temptation, and chase away Satan from us.
—THOMAS MANTON[1]

True believers have a peace of which the unbeliever knows nothing. They are also at war in a manner in which the unbeliever has no experience. Believers have objective peace with God. "Therefore being justified by faith, we have peace with God through our Lord Jesus Christ" (Rom. 5:1). Subjectively, they have the peace of God within them, guarding their hearts and minds through Christ Jesus (Phil. 4:7). This peace is not an absence of war; it is in the midst of war. Peace with God means war with His enemies.

This war is objective, as the believer daily battles the world and the devil. But it is also subjective—internal—as a struggle against the flesh. Though Christ has made His people "more than conquerors" in this battle (Rom. 8:37), we often feel weary and beaten down, battered and bruised, by our combat against the three-headed monster of sin. We must daily face this beast and its

1. Thomas Manton, *Sermons Upon the CXIX. Psalm* in *The Complete Works of Thomas Manton* (London: James Nisbet, 1871), 8:62.

uncanny strength, which is beyond that which mere mortal flesh is capable of subduing. Our recourse must be to the power of God. His strength is made perfect in our weakness (2 Cor. 12:9). We should keep in our view the hope that God has promised victory in this battle—not necessarily in every skirmish, but in the war as a whole.

The joy and the peace, the battles and the warfare, fluctuate and alternate in our conscious experience of them. Spiritual strife persists throughout the marathon of the Christian race. It is a battle to be a Christian. The believer, contrary to the sanctified desires within him, laments that he succumbs to one temptation or another. He confesses with Paul in Romans 7:15, "For [the good that] I would, that do I not: but [the evil that] I hate, that do I," and cries out: "Oh wretched man that I am!" (Rom. 7:24). What a battle the struggle against sin can be!

John Bunyan called it a holy war that takes place within "Mansoul." It's a war that focuses on the gates of the city: the eyegate and the eargate, through which Satan brings a host of temptations and sin to get the believer to fall.[2] The Puritans were keen on the topic of spiritual warfare. Their burden was to equip believers to engage in battle victoriously. In this chapter, we'll consider how the Puritans help to equip us in the battle against the world, the flesh, and the devil.

The Battle against the World

In one sense, everyone who is truly in Christ has already overcome the world by faith. First John 5:4 says, "For whatsoever is born of God overcometh the world: and this is the victory that overcometh the world, even our faith." But Scripture also calls us to thrive in grace by striving to overcome this world with faithful endurance (Rev. 2:7, 17, 26; 3:12, 21). True faith *will* persevere and

---

2. John Bunyan, *The Holy War* (Ross-shire, Scotland: Christian Focus, 1993), 21.

endure (1 Peter 1:5), but true faith also *must* persevere and endure (Matt. 24:13). The promise is certain, but it does not abdicate our responsibility. In this struggle, we are charged to keep ourselves "unspotted from the world" (James 1:27).

The Christian life is not a middle way between two extremes but a narrow way between precipices (Matt. 7:13–14). It involves living by faith through self-denial (Luke 9:23), waging holy war in the midst of a hostile world (2 Cor. 10:4). We either love the world or we love the Father (1 John 2:15). The two loves are exclusive. But the world will not cease to attack us by means of attracting us with its allurements and opposing us with its persecutions.

For the Christian who would like to learn about how to overcome the world, scarcely a better resource can be consulted than William Greenhill's (1598–1671) *Stop Loving the World*.[3] Greenhill takes up 1 John 2:15 for his text and begins by defining the world and what it means to love it (in the negative sense): "Love not the *world*" means: "Do not love the creatures of the world, the customs and fashions of the world, or the splendor, pomp, glory, and worship of the world."[4]

But what does it mean to "love" in 1 John 2:15? In what sense must we not "love" the world? Greenhill gives a tenfold explanation. To love the world is: (1) to highly esteem the world, holding it in high account, giving it priority above the call of Christ; (2) to have one's thoughts fixed on the world, for "what a person loves, their thoughts are much upon"; (3) to have strong desires after the world; (4) to set one's heart and affections upon the world; (5) to "employ most of our strength, in, on, and about the things of the world"; (6) to be on "watch" for "all opportunities and occasions to get the things of the world," such as securing possessions as our treasure; (7) to eagerly endure great hardships for the world while God's ordinances, like worshiping on the Lord's Day, are

---

3. William Greenhill, *Stop Loving the World* (Grand Rapids: Reformation Heritage Books, 2011).
4. Greenhill, *Stop Loving the World*, 5.

found burdensome; (8) to favor the world, as manifested in constant worldly speech; (9) to mourn and lament over the loss of merely earthly things, like estates or names or earthly privileges; (10) to resolve to be rich and filled with earthly abundance as one's priority in life.[5]

Though we must not love the world, Greenhill explains that we must not "totally cast off the world and have nothing to do with it." We should have a "legitimate interaction with the world."[6] We do this by studying "the world and the works of God in the world." God's works are honorable, "sought out of all them that have pleasure therein" (Ps. 111:2).[7] By studying general revelation, we can learn truths about God and marvel at His greatness. We may also "pray for the things of this world,"[8] whatever we may have need of as far as our bodily existence is concerned. We must also pursue vocation in this world, including work and marriage.[9] Finally, we may also, as 1 Corinthians 7:31 says, be people who "use this world, not as abusing it."[10] Christians have a holy, heavenly calling that transcends the vanity and temporality of this world.[11]

Greenhill offers practical wisdom on how to use but not abuse the world. He gives six lines of advice:

1. "Use all things for the end that God has made them." Proverbs 16:4 says, "The Lord hath made all things for himself." We should use created things, whether our bodies, affections, or possessions, for God's honor and glory.[12]

2. "Walk with God in the use of the world and answer God's call." Like Enoch, we must walk with God, heeding to our Lord as the One to whom we are supremely devoted in our

---

5. Greenhill, *Stop Loving the World*, 3–14.
6. Greenhill, *Stop Loving the World*, 29.
7. Greenhill, *Stop Loving the World*, 29.
8. Greenhill, *Stop Loving the World*, 31.
9. Greenhill, *Stop Loving the World*, 32.
10. Greenhill, *Stop Loving the World*, 33.
11. Greenhill, *Stop Loving the World*, 15.
12. Greenhill, *Stop Loving the World*, 33.

calling, looking heavenward rather than being earthbound in our thought patterns.[13]

3. "*Use the things of this world to promote spiritual good in ourselves and others.*" For instance, make friends with unrighteous mammon rather than stepping on others to obtain personal gain.[14]

4. "*Use the world slightly and consider the things of God and of my soul as my main business.*" Labor to store up a good eternal condition, not a temporal earthly one.[15]

5. "*Use the world in moderation, keeping your affections in check.*" Our desires and affections for everything in this world must be moderated and kept in check under the supreme love of the Father.[16]

6. "*Give a good and cheerful account to God concerning what we have had in the world.*" God allocates to each person their own portion. We should use our portion according to the principles of good stewardship so that we can give an account to God in the last day with joy.[17]

This list is very helpful to use as a checklist to take personal spiritual inventory. Ask yourself, "Do these six directions describe my heart's disposition toward the world?"

The rest of Greenhill's treatise gives counsel on how to love the creature lawfully without loving the world illicitly and issues exhortations to break off the love of the world and cherish the things of God. He also furnishes motives for why we should cast off the love of the world in the pursuit of God's glory. Finally, he extols the love of God as the supreme affection that displaces inordinate earthly affection: "The more our love for God grows,

---

13. Greenhill, *Stop Loving the World*, 34.
14. Greenhill, *Stop Loving the World*, 34–35.
15. Greenhill, *Stop Loving the World*, 35.
16. Greenhill, *Stop Loving the World*, 35–36.
17. Greenhill, *Stop Loving the World*, 36.

the more our hearts will be estranged from the world…. Look on the beauties of God, for the excellencies of God are such as would ravish a man's soul and draw it up to Him."[18]

I would like to encourage you to take the Puritans' writings and make them practical as helps to faith and holiness. Learn to read them slowly, deliberately, with prayer and meditation, and you'll get the greatest profit from them. For example, Greenhill's ten indicators can be used as a practical means of self-examination. Take them to prayer and meditation and ask yourself whether you may have some inordinate affection for the world. Use them to expose your shortcomings and pray that the Lord would shed more of His love abroad in your heart by the Holy Spirit (Rom. 5:5).

The Puritans help us in practical, experiential piety because they so clearly explain the truths they take up, while they facilitate to us so many practical helps in our pursuit of the "holiness, without which no man shall see the Lord" (Heb. 12:14). In your battle against the world, read other books, like Jeremiah Burroughs's *A Treatise on Earthly-Mindedness* or his book titled *Moses' Self-Denial*.[19] Make the Puritans your companions; fellowship with them while on your journey from this world to that which is to come. Speaking out of the depths of their own struggles and conflicts, they are like seasoned war veterans who return from the field to inform new soldiers of what lies ahead, that we may navigate the battlefield of this world victoriously.

---

18. Greenhill, *Stop Loving the World*, 72–73.

19. Jeremiah Burroughs, *A Treatise on Earthly-Mindedness* (1649; repr., Grand Rapids: Soli Deo Gloria, 2013); *Moses' Self-Denial* (1641; repr., Grand Rapids: Soli Deo Gloria, 2010). Burroughs is easier to read than many other Puritans. He is an eminent example of the Puritan "plain style" of preaching, and his books are basically his printed sermons that were spoken to common congregations. Many are familiar with his *Rare Jewel of Christian Contentment*, an excellent treatment of what it means to rest content in the Lord (a much needed topic today!). But his other works are just as practical and easy to read and are full of experiential theology that may be put to the service of one's pursuit of holiness.

The Battle against the Flesh

In Romans 7:14–23, Paul lets us into the inmost being of his soul—into that inner, continual conflict between the Spirit and the flesh, between the contrary principles that abode in the heart of the great apostle—between the new nature and the remains of the old nature. Verses 22–23 read, "For I delight in the law of God after the inward man: but I see another law in my members, warring against the law of my mind, and bringing me into captivity to the law of sin which is in my members."

The apostle speaks of two laws: the law of God and the law of sin. God's law, summarized in the Ten Commandments, is holy, just, and good (Rom. 7:12). Since this law is spiritual (Rom. 7:14), the Spirit of God acquiesces with it and asserts His sanctifying influence in accordance with it. But the law of sin is radically opposed to it, as an operational principle that bucks against it, like an untamed horse against its rider. These two laws stand contrary to one another and war within the believer. The law of sin cannot be tamed; it must be put down. The only remedy for it is death, or, as Owen famously put it, to kill it.

The most well-known Puritan works on battling the sin within us are the trilogy of John Owen: *On the Mortification of Sin, Of Temptation*, and *Of Indwelling Sin*.[20] Owen, with his keen insight into human nature, penetrates the inner workings of indwelling sin. He defines "the law of sin" as "a powerful and effectual indwelling principle, inclining and pressing unto actions agreeable and suitable unto its own nature."[21] Commenting on its being called a "law," he says, "there is an exceeding efficacy and power in the remains of indwelling sin in believers, with a constant working toward evil."[22] Indwelling sin is always working, always exerting

---

20. This trilogy is published as a single book for modern readers in John Owen, *Overcoming Sin and Temptation*, ed. Kelly M. Kapic and Justin Taylor (Wheaton, Ill.: Crossway, 2015).

21. Owen, *Overcoming Sin and Temptation*, 234. Italics removed.

22. Owen, *Overcoming Sin and Temptation*, 234. Italics removed.

itself, and its influence is effectual in that it is successful in producing its effective result, which is to tempt and ensnare the believer. In hypocrites, this law of sin has dominion. In genuine believers, it may be strong, and it may occasionally exert itself with uncanny force, but it is definitively weakened and progressively mortified, and the dominion of it has been broken by regenerating grace. The Christian life must engage in the holy warfare of a continual and ever-increasing mortification of sin by the means of grace, empowered by the Spirit. The flesh never ceases to drag us down.

The term "flesh," used in this way, refers not to human nature as created by God but conceptualizes human nature as enslaved and corrupted by sin, particularly in regard to the principle of sin that operates within. Because of this inbred corruption, we all stand in need of a sovereign, supernatural work of omnipotent grace. Jesus spoke of the flesh as an antithetical, inherent principle when he said, "That which is born of the flesh is flesh; and that which is born of the Spirit is spirit" (John 3:6). William Bates (1625–1699) explains that, due to the flesh's corruption, these words stress the absolute necessity of regeneration:

> The flesh is a corrupt principle, and accordingly the Natural Man is wholly carnal in his propensions, operations and end. The disease is turned into his constitution. He is dead to the spiritual life, to the actions and enjoyments that are proper to it: nay, there is in him a surviving principle of enmity to that life; not only a mortal coldness to God, but a stiff aversation from him, a perpetual resistance and impatience of the divine presence, that would disturb his voluptuous enjoyments. The exercises of heaven would be as the torments of hell to him, while in the midst of those pure joys his inward inclinations vehemently run into the lowest lees of sensuality. And therefore till this contrariety, so deep and predominant in an unholy person, be removed, it is utterly impossible he should enjoy God with satisfaction.[23]

23. William Bates, *The Four Last Things: viz. Death, Judgment, Heaven, Hell,*

The gospel is powerful to save and transform because it is the remedy for a fallen condition that nothing but the power of God can change. In equipping us in the battle against the flesh, the Puritans point us continually to the power of the Holy Spirit unleashed by the gospel. Though the Christian no longer walks in the flesh, the flesh remains present. As only the Spirit can produce spiritual life out of our dead fleshly condition, only the Spirit can sanctify the believer to overcome the vestiges of sin's remaining corruption. Regeneration and ongoing renovation are supernatural acts of the Spirit's grace.

The Puritans didn't just point out the nature of indwelling sin. They didn't wallow in a "wretched man mentality" (as some have pejoratively put it), but their spirituality wisely demonstrates a practical realism combined with a hopeful idealism. While Romans 8 presents an idealistic picture of the Christian life, Romans 7 presents the Christian life with a down-to-earth realism. The Puritans taught that we need to hold both in the proper tension and balance to have a sound understanding of the Christian life. We can learn from them to have a sober self-assessment while not losing sight of the glories of the gospel.

Christians today often underestimate the power of sin. In all our talk about being "gospel-centered," we must not lose sight of the reality of the sin that dwells within us. Our main focus, to be sure, should be on the gospel. The Puritans spoke much of meditating on the glories of Christ, the sufficiency of the gospel, and the wonders of heaven. But if we have a superficial view of the power of indwelling sin, we will have a superficial view of how the gospel effectively equips us to crucify it. Too many today mince words when they talk about the flesh and indwelling sin. We must not paint up and pamper that which is putrefied and in need of being mortified.

Practically Considered and Applied, in *The Whole Works of the Rev. William Bates,* ed. W. Farmer (Harrisonburg, Va.: Sprinkle Publications, 1990), 3:420–21.

Thomas Watson didn't mince words when he warned about the "enemy within":

> The flesh is a worse enemy than the devil, it is a bosom-traitor; an enemy within is worst. If there were no devil to tempt, the flesh would be another Eve, to tempt to the forbidden fruit. O take heed of giving way to it! Whence is all our discontent but from the fleshy part? The flesh puts us upon the immoderate pursuit of the world; it consults for ease and plenty, and if it be not satisfied, then discontents begin to arise. O let it not have the reins! Martyr the flesh! In spiritual things the flesh is a sluggard, in secular things an horse-leech, crying, "give, give." The flesh is an enemy to suffering; it will sooner make a man a courtier, than a martyr. O keep it under! Put its neck under Christ's yoke,—stretch and nail it to his cross,—never let a Christian look for contentment in his spirit, till there be confinement in his flesh![24]

Now, that's a classic Puritan exhortation! May it not fall upon us as music to our ears, but as a sword to our hearts, to cut out our indwelling impurity and purge our corruption at its root.

Watson is speaking relatively when he says the flesh is a worse enemy to us than the devil. The reason is that although the devil is outside us, the flesh is within us. But the Puritans never underestimated the power of their personal foe, which leads us to consider the third enemy we war against in this daily battle.

The Battle against the Devil

The Puritans believed that a literal and personal devil is the arch-enemy of the people of God.[25] That he is a personal being can

---

24. Thomas Watson, *The Select Works of the Rev. Thomas Watson, Comprising His Celebrated Body of Divinity, in a Series of Lectures on the Shorter Catechism, and Various Sermons and Treatises* (New York: Robert Carter & Brothers, 1855), 730.

25. This section has been adapted, with some modification, from Joel R. Beeke, *Striving Against Satan: Knowing the Enemy—His Weakness, His Strategy, His Defeat* (Bridgend, Wales: Bryntirion Press, 1996). Used with permission.

be discerned from his names in Scripture. *Satan* derives from a Hebrew word that means "an accuser or adversary, one who resists." The term is used nineteen times in the Old Testament, fourteen of which are in Job 1 and 2. The New Testament most often refers to Satan as "the devil" (*diabolos*). That term means traducer or slanderer. He slanders man to God, he slanders God to man, and he slanders man to man. Other New Testament names include the accuser (Rev. 12:10), the adversary (1 Peter 5:8), Apollyon (Rev. 9:11), Beelzebub (Matt. 12:24), Belial (2 Cor. 6:15), the dragon (Rev. 12:7), the god of this world (2 Cor. 4:4), the prince of the power of the air (Eph. 2:2), the prince of this world (John 12:31), the serpent (Rev. 20:2), the tempter (Matt. 4:3), and a roaring lion (1 Peter 5:8).

Some are obsessed with Satan; they think they see demons lurking everywhere. The Puritans were more balanced. Millions of others in modern civilization, however, don't believe the devil exists at all. This attitude has even permeated the church. Spurgeon said in his day, "Certain theologians, nowadays, do not believe in the existence of Satan.... But, beloved, the power of Satan in a Christian man's life is a force with which he must reckon, or he may fail through ignorance."[26]

The Puritans became greatly familiar with the strategies and devices of Satan. They wrote frequently and with great depth on spiritual warfare. Some works that have recently been reprinted include:

• Thomas Brooks's *Precious Remedies Against Satan's Devices*, a well-known classic that has often been reprinted by Banner of Truth

26. Charles H. Spurgeon, "The Warnings and the Rewards of the Word of God," in *The Metropolitan Tabernacle Pulpit Sermons* (London: Passmore & Alabaster, 1890), 36:160–161.

- Richard Gilpin's (1625–1700) *A Treatise on Satan's Temptations*, a 500-page classic recently reprinted by Soli Deo Gloria

- William Spurstowe's (1605–1666) *The Wiles of Satan*, a rare but helpful little work, recently reprinted by Soli Deo Gloria

- William Gurnall's (1616–1679) *The Christian in Complete Armour*, a detailed treatise on Ephesians 6:10–20, reprinted by Banner of Truth

- Thomas Goodwin's *A Child of Light Walking in Darkness*, which has a most helpful section on Satan's activity in our spiritual darkness (*Works of Goodwin*, 3:256–288).

There is a gold mine of practical wisdom in these writings on how to thrive in grace by recognizing and resisting Satan's attacks.

We need to fight Satan by reclaiming biblical spiritual warfare, as set forth by Paul in Ephesians 6:10–20. As Gurnall said: "It is not enough to have grace, but this grace must be kept in exercise. The Christian's armor is made to be worn; no laying down, or putting off our armor, till we have done our warfare, and finished our course."[27] We should be on defensive guard and employ biblical strategies in our battle with the devil. We must build an unyielding defense and an attacking offense.

Building an Unyielding Defense
Ephesians 6:14–17a says, "Stand therefore, having your loins girt about with truth, and having on the breastplate of righteousness; and your feet shod with the preparation of the gospel of peace; above all, taking the shield of faith, wherewith ye shall be able to quench all the fiery darts of the wicked. And take the helmet of salvation."

---

27. William Gurnall, *The Christian in Complete Armour* (1662–1665; repr., Edinburgh: Banner of Truth, 2002), 1:63–64.

"Stand therefore," we are told. Thomas Manton points out that "It is a military word.... The word intimateth perseverance."[28] It means to take a fighting position, to be prepared for battle, resolute to endure, whatever the enemy may hurl at you. Peter exhorts to this very thing when he says, "Be sober, be vigilant; because your adversary the devil, as a roaring lion, walketh about, seeking whom he may devour: whom resist stedfast in the faith" (1 Pet. 5:8–9a). Satan was "seeking" to devour the saints thousands of years ago; he tirelessly continues to seek them out today. Thomas Boston warned, "Satan never ceases to seek your destruction."[29] He is always scheming, always prowling, always lurking, waiting for the opportune time to pounce upon the child of God and sink his fangs into the jugular of our spiritual vitality.

In our defensive stance we are to be watchful with vigilant spiritual sobriety. As the Lord said, "Watch and pray, that ye enter not into temptation" (Matt. 26:41). Jonathan Edwards graphically explains what it means to "watch":

> We had need to keep and watch over our hearts with all dili-gence, because Satan diligently watches over them. We had need to be watching day and night over our hearts, as a man would watch a treasure that is carefully watched by thieves.... As wild beasts are wont to watch for their prey, to lurk priv-ily in some secret place that they might seize their prey unawares, as wolves watch the fold; so doth the devil watch over our hearts, that he may pervert and confound them. 'Tis for his crafty, hidden, secret way of working men's destruc-tion that he is represented by a serpent, which is wont to bite the careless traveler before ever he is aware, or has any notice. The devil watches for such opportunities, as when men are asleep, most careless and least upon their guard.[30]

28. Thomas Manton, *Eighteen Sermons on the Second Chapter of the Second Epistle to the Thessalonians,* in *Works,* 3:122.

29. Thomas Boston, *Discourses on Prayer,* in *The Whole Works of Thomas Boston,* ed. Samuel M'Millan (Aberdeen: George and Robert King, 1852), 11:19.

30. Jonathan Edwards, "Keeping Our Hearts with All Diligence," in *Jonathan*

Satan strategically strikes in our moments of greatest weakness. Edwards explained, "The devil is ready at hand to take every occasion to see when corruption is uppermost, to see when men are in worldly frames, or when they are in passionate frames, or in sensual frames, or when men are in the most tempting circumstances, and is careful to make his advantage of it."[31] The times when we least feel like standing our ground are precisely when we need to do so most!

Many of the articles of the armor of God serve defensive purposes. Each one is critical, but an adequate explanation of them all would go beyond our present confinements in this little book. For a thorough exposition of each piece of armor, see William Gurnall's *Christian in Complete Armour*. This book is unsurpassed in its detail, theological depth, and experiential applicability.

Building an Attacking Offense

It is not enough to stand our ground. We must also advance! Jesus said that the gates of hell will not prevail against the church (Matt. 16:18). In antiquity, the gates of a city were the part that was under siege by attacking armies on the offense. Manton said, "In the spiritual conflict we need weapons not only defensive but offensive; not only the shield of faith, but the sword of the Spirit, that we may destroy and slay sin, and withstand temptation, and chase away Satan from us."[32] The church is to battle Satan by prayer and the Word. Ephesians 6:17b–18a says, "Take…the sword of the Spirit, which is the word of God: praying always with all prayer."

The Word of God gives us clear directions, powerful motives, rich encouragements, and instructive examples that equip us well for confronting Satan. Intimately acquaint yourself with the Bible

---

Edwards Sermons, ed. Wilson H. Kimnach (New Haven, Conn.: Jonathan Edwards Center at Yale University, 1728–1729), Proverbs 4:23.

31. Edwards, "Keeping Our Hearts with All Diligence," in *Jonathan Edwards Sermons*, Proverbs 4:23.

32. Manton, *Sermons Upon the CXIX. Psalm,* in *Works*, 8:62.

by studying and memorizing it daily. That will help keep God's sword sharp in your hand. Keep that sword polished and bright by living the Bible's truths each day. Keep the sword ready at all times through constant prayer. Speak out and bear witness to Scripture truth. Carry the light of God's Word into a dark world, shining it into every dark corner. In dependence on the Spirit, use the sword of the Bible. Stand your ground against Satan, to assail him, to run at him, to rout him, and to drive him from the field. It will never fail you, not even in the thick of the battle with Satan, as Bunyan so poignantly tells of Christian while in the valley of humiliation:

> Christian began to despair of life: but as God would have it, while Apollyon was fetching of his last blow, thereby to make a full end of this good man, Christian nimbly stretched out his hand for his sword, and caught it, saying, "Rejoice not against me, O mine enemy: when I fall, I shall arise" (Micah 7:8); and with that gave him a deadly thrust, which made him give back, as one that had received his mortal wound. Christian perceiving that, made at him again, saying, "Nay, in all these things we are more than conquerors, through Him that loved us" (Rom. 8:37). And with that Apollyon spread forth his dragon's wings, and sped him away, that Christian for a season saw him no more (James 4:7).[33]

Prayer is the second offensive weapon against Satan. It is critical. "Prayer keeps the heart open to God, but shut to sin; it is a key which unlocks God's treasures of mercy,"[34] says Watson. And Gurnall writes, "Prayer is the channel in which the stream of divine grace, blessing, and comfort runs from God the fountain into the cistern of their hearts."[35]

Because of our weakness in prayer, we often fall in battle. Spurgeon said, "That battle which commences without holy reliance

---

33. John Bunyan, *The Pilgrim's Progress,* in *The Works of John Bunyan*, ed. George Offor (1854; repr., Edinburgh: Banner of Truth, 1991), 3:113.

34. Thomas Watson, *Puritan Gems; or, Wise and Holy Sayings of the Rev. Thomas Watson, A.M.*, ed. John Adey (London: J. Snow, and Ward and Co., 1850), 107.

35. Gurnall, *Christian in Complete Armour*, 2:500.

upon God, shall certainly end in a terrible rout. Many men might be Christian victors, if they had known how to use the all prevailing weapon of prayer; but forgetting this they have gone to the fight and they have been worsted right easily."[36]

Every piece of Christian armor is useless without it. Prayer is like oil. Just as every part of an engine is useless without oil, so every part of Christian warfare is vain without prayer.[37] Fighting Satan without prayer would be like David fighting Goliath in his own name rather than in the name of the Lord of hosts. All our abilities, all our learning, all our skills, will be to no avail against Satan if we do not have the power of Christ upon us.

The church needs to learn to snap out of her sleepy, halfhearted, lethargic prayers and start praying warfare prayers that pierce the heavens with earnest cries for help in this battle. "That prayer is most likely to pierce heaven which first pierces one's own heart."[38] When Moses held up his hands, Israel prevailed, but when he grew weary and let them down, Amalek prevailed (Ex. 17:11). We will prevail in this conflict with Satan only if we are "lifting up holy hands" unto God in prayer continually (1 Tim. 2:8). We'll explore what the Puritans taught about prayer more in the next chapter. As we conclude this chapter, let's take heed to these stirring words from an old hymn by Charlotte Elliot (1789–1871):

> Christian, seek not yet repose,
> Hear thy gracious Savior say;
> Thou art in the midst of foes:
>   Watch and pray.
>
> Principalities and powers,
> Mustering their unseen array,

---

36. Charles H. Spurgeon, "All-Sufficiency Magnified," in *The New Park Street Pulpit Sermons* (London: Passmore & Alabaster, 1860), 6:483.

37. Gurnall said, "The Christian's armour will rust except it be furbished and scoured with the oil of prayer." *Christian in Complete Armour,* 2:288.

38. Watson, *Puritan Gems,* 109.

Wait for thy unguarded hours:
  Watch and pray.

Gird thy heavenly armor on,
Wear it ever night and day;
Ambushed lies the evil one:
  Watch and pray.

Hear the victors who o'ercame,
Still they mark each warrior's way;
All with one sweet voice exclaim,
  Watch and pray.

Hear, above all, hear thy Lord,
Him thou lovest to obey;
Hide within thy heart His word:
  Watch and pray.

Watch, as if on that alone
Hung the issue of the day;
Pray, that help may be sent down
  Watch and pray.[39]

---

39. Charlotte Elliot, "Christian Seek Not Yet Repose" (1836).

Questions for Reflection and Discussion

1. What is the difference between loving the world and using the world? How could the Puritans' wisdom change your ways of interacting with the world?

2. The Puritans wrote with a combination of practical, down-to-earth realism about the nature and ongoing influence of the flesh and indwelling sin, as well as hopeful idealism rooted in the truth of the gospel and the power of God's Spirit. Why do we need both? Do you tend to gravitate more toward realism or idealism?

3. Are you faithfully putting on the whole armor of God? What practical steps do you need to take to build an "unyielding defense" and an "attacking offense" in your battle against the world, the flesh, and the devil?

8

THE PURITANS
Inspire Our Hearts to Seek God's Face in Prayer

Pray often, for prayer is a shield to the soul,
a sacrifice to God, and a scourge for Satan.
—JOHN BUNYAN[1]

The Scripture says that Elijah "prayed earnestly"[2]: "Elias was a man subject to like passions as we are, and he prayed earnestly that it might not rain: and it rained not on the earth by the space of three years and six months" (James 5:17). The KJV marginal notes provide the alternate translation that the prophet "prayed in his prayer." In other words, his prayers were more than a formal exercise; he poured himself into his praying. You might call this "prayerful praying." Bible commentator Alexander Ross notes that this idiom communicates intensity; in contrast, "A man may pray with his lips and yet not pray with an intense desire of the soul."[3]

1. John Bunyan, *Mr. John Bunyan's Dying Sayings,* in *The Works of John Bunyan,* ed. George Offor (1854; repr., Edinburgh: Banner of Truth, 1991), 1:65.

2. This chapter is abridged and adapted, with some modifications, from Joel R. Beeke, "Prayerful Praying Today," in *Taking Hold of God: Reformed and Puritan Perspectives on Prayer,* ed. Joel R. Beeke and Brian G. Najapfour (Grand Rapids: Reformation Heritage Books, 2011), 223–40. Used with permission.

3. Alexander Ross, *The Epistles of James and John,* The New International Commentary on the New Testament (Grand Rapids: Eerdmans, 1954), 102.

After studying the prayer lives of the Reformers and Puritans, I am convinced that the greatest shortcoming in today's church is the lack of such "prayerful prayer." We fail to use heaven's greatest weapon as we should. Personally, domestically, and congregationally, the prayer we engage in is often more prayerless than prayerful. All Christians are called to pray (Col. 4:2). Is anything more essential, yet more neglected among us, than prayer? The giants of church history dwarf us in true prayer. They were prayerful men who knew how to take hold of God in prayer (Isa. 64:7), being possessed by the Spirit of grace and supplication. They were Daniels in private and public prayer.

Our prayerlessness is the more tragic because of the tremendous potential of prayer. Thomas Brooks wrote, "Ah! How often, Christians, hath God kissed you at the beginning of prayer, and spoke peace to you in the midst of prayer, and filled you with joy and assurance, upon the close of prayer!"[4] The wife of Joseph Alleine said of her husband:

> At the time of his health, he did rise constantly at or before four of the clock, and on the Sabbath sooner, if he did wake. He would be much troubled if he heard smiths, or shoemakers, or such tradesmen, at work at their trades before he was in his duties with God; saying to me often, "O how this noise shames me! Doth not my Master deserve more than theirs?" From four till eight he spent in prayer, holy contemplation, and singing of psalms, which he much delighted in, and did daily practice alone, as well as in his family.[5]

In this chapter, let us consider what the Puritans taught about thriving in grace by cultivating a healthy prayer life. If we are faithful in our efforts to acquire more of the gift and grace of true

---

4. Thomas Brooks, *Heaven on Earth,* in *The Works of Thomas Brooks*, ed. Alexander B. Grosart (1861–1867; repr., Edinburgh: Banner of Truth, 2001), 2:369.
5. Richard Baxter, et al, *The Life and Letters of Joseph Alleine* (repr., Grand Rapids: Reformation Heritage Books, 2003), 106.

prayer, we can be sure God will help us to "take hold of" Him (Isa. 64:7) as we seek His face.

It is far easier to generate guilt about prayerlessness than to solve the problem. It is far easier to feel bad about powerless prayer than to repent and obey. But, as Paul says in 1 Timothy 4:7, "Exercise thyself rather unto godliness." He adds in 1 Timothy 6:12, "Fight the good fight of faith, lay hold on eternal life." I thus plead with you, based on the imperatives of Scripture and the example of the Puritans and other godly Christians through the ages, to urgently seek a more fervent and faithful prayer life. This will require you to take hold of yourself and God. The Puritans were masters of prayer, and they offer helpful counsel on how to be prayerful in our praying.

Take Hold of Yourself for Prayer

Prayerful praying does not happen automatically. It's hard work! George Swinnock said, "Dost thou labour in prayer? Col. 4:12, *i.e.*, wrestle with God, as the word imports, bending and straining every joint of the new man in the soul, that they may all help to prevail with God."[6] It requires self-control, which is not a legalistic mandate but a fruit of the Spirit prompted by the cross of Jesus Christ (Gal. 5:22–24). We must look to Christ as the vine who can produce good fruit in us, get a grip on ourselves, and engage in disciplined prayer.

David took hold of himself in prayer. He did not wallow in depression but engaged in self-examination, saying in Psalm 42:5, "Why art thou cast down, O my soul? and why art thou disquieted in me? hope thou in God: for I shall yet praise him for the help of his countenance." David did not sink into thanklessness but rose to thank God in the midst of his troubles. In Psalm 103:2 he says, "Bless the LORD, O my soul, and forget not all his benefits."

---

6. George Swinnock, *Heaven and Hell Epitomised,* in *The Works of George Swinnock,* (Edinburgh: James Nichol, 1868), 3:303.

Consider the following seven principles of how to take hold of yourself for prayer.

1. *Remember the value of prayer.* Seek to realize the value of unanswered as well as answered prayer. William Carey (1761–1834) labored as a missionary in India for eight years before baptizing the first convert from Hinduism to Christ.[7] Yet in those years Carey learned to live for the glory of God alone. He wrote, "I feel that it is good to commit my soul, my body, and my all, into the hands of God. Then the world appears little, the promises great, and God an all-sufficient portion."[8] God's delay became marrow for Carey's soul. "You must distinguish between delays and denials," said Thomas Brooks.[9] William Bridge went even deeper, saying, "A praying man can never be very miserable, whatever his condition be, for he has the ear of God; the Spirit within to indite, a Friend in heaven to present, and God Himself to receive his desires. It is a mercy to pray, even though I never receive the mercy prayed for."[10]

But if unanswered prayer is sweet, how much sweeter is answered prayer! "Good prayers never come weeping home," wrote Joseph Hall (1574–1656); "I am sure I shall receive either what I ask or what I should ask."[11] God knows what is best for His children. He never denies us anything that we ask for in humble submission and according to His will. So pray on. Refuse to leave the Lord alone. Keep before you the encouraging words of Thomas Watson: "The angel fetched Peter out of prison, but it was prayer that fetched the angel."[12] Beg the Lord to bring back the days of

7. Timothy George, *Faithful Witness: The Life and Mission of William Carey* (Birmingham, Ala.: New Hope, 1991), 131.

8. George, *Faithful Witness*, 104.

9. Brooks, *Heaven on Earth*, in *Works*, 2:371.

10. William Bridge, *A Lifting Up for the Downcast* (1648; repr., Edinburgh: Banner of Truth, 1990), 55.

11. Cited in John Blanchard, comp., *The Complete Gathered Gold* (Darlington, U.K.: Evangelical Press, 2006), 455.

12. Thomas Watson, *A Divine Cordial* (1663; repr., Wilmington, Del.: Sovereign Grace Publishers, 1972), 18.

John Knox (c. 1514–1572), when his enemies dreaded his prayers more than the armies of ten thousand men.

2. Maintain the priority of prayer. Apart from the Lord, we can do nothing (John 15:5). John Bunyan wrote, "You can do more than pray, after you have prayed, but you cannot do more than pray until you have prayed."[13] He also said, "Pray often, for prayer is a shield to the soul, a sacrifice to God, and a scourge for Satan."[14] As a primary means of grace in conjunction with the Word, nothing is more pertinent to the life of faith. Thomas Boston said, "Prayer is a duty of natural religion, and by God's appointment is one of the chief means by which Christ communicates the benefits of redemption to sinners."[15] Prayer is like a key that opens heaven's treasure chest, which is full of the riches Christ secured for His people.

Let us then value prayer as the chief means to assist us in our Christian duties, reserving time for prayer regularly, to raise up petitions before the throne of grace concerning our ongoing needs. Struggle to avoid prayerless praying, whether in private devotion or in public prayer. Even if your prayers seem lifeless, do not stop praying. Dullness may be beyond your immediate ability to overcome, but refusing to pray at all is the fruit of presumption, self-sufficiency, and slothfulness. When even the outward form of prayer is gone, all is gone. It is easy to pray when you are like a sailboat gliding forward in a favoring wind. But you must also pray when you are like an icebreaker smashing your way through an arctic sea one foot at a time. No matter what, keep prayer your priority.

---

13. Cited in I. D. E. Thomas, comp., *The Golden Treasury of Puritan Quotations* (Chicago: Moody Press, 1975), 210.

14. John Bunyan, *Mr. John Bunyan's Dying Sayings,* in *The Works of John Bunyan,* ed. George Offor (1854; repr., Edinburgh: Banner of Truth, 1991), 1:65.

15. Thomas Boston, *An Illustration of the Doctrines of the Christian Religion,* in *The Whole Works of Thomas Boston,* ed. Samuel M'Millan (Aberdeen: George and Robert King, 1848), 2:526.

3. Speak with sincerity in prayer. Psalm 62:8 says, "Trust in him at all times; ye people, pour out your heart before him: God is a refuge for us." To pray with your mouth what is not truly in your heart is hypocrisy—unless you are confessing the coldness of your heart and crying out for heart-warming grace. Bunyan said, "When thou prayest, rather let thy heart be without words, than thy words without a heart."[16] Sometimes a sincere prayer, such as Psalm 119, is long and carefully crafted. Sometimes a sincere prayer, such as Luke 18:13, is quite simple: "God be merciful to me a sinner." Either way, settle for nothing less than sincerity in your prayer.

Be encouraged to strive for sincerity in prayer by these words of Thomas Brooks:

> God looks not at the elegancy of your prayers, to see how neat they are; nor yet at the geometry of your prayers to see how long they are; nor yet at the arithmetic of your prayers, to see how many they are; nor yet at the music of your prayers, nor yet at the sweetness of your voice, nor yet at the logic of your prayers; but at the sincerity of your prayers, how hearty they are. There is no prayer acknowledged, approved, accepted, recorded, or rewarded by God, but that wherein the heart is sincerely and wholly. The true mother would not have the child divided. As God loves a broken and a contrite heart, so he loathes a divided heart.[17]

4. Cultivate a continual spirit of prayer. "Pray without ceasing," says Paul in 1 Thessalonians 5:17. This refers to the spirit, habit, and condition of prayer rather than to the physical act of prayer. It refers more to praying with your hat on and your eyes open than to petitioning in private. Thomas Brooks said, "A man must always pray habitually, though not actually; he must have his heart in a praying disposition in all estates and conditions, in prosperity and adversity, in health and sickness, in strength and weakness, in

---

16. Bunyan, *Dying Sayings,* in *Works,* 1:65.
17. Brooks, *The Privy Key of Prayer,* in *Works,* 2:256.

wealth and wants, in life and death."[18] Thomas Manton preached
to his congregation on the vital importance of frequent praying as
an expression of fellowship with God:

> [Prayer] is the converse of a loving soul with God, the near-
> est familiarity which a soul dwelling in flesh can have with
> him. Now acts of friendship and communion must not be
> rare and unfrequent, but constant and often, therefore called
> an acquainting ourselves with God: Job 22:21, "Acquaint now
> thyself with him, and be at peace." Acquaintance implieth
> frequent commerce and intercourse. Men that often visit one
> another, and meet together are acquainted. Prayer is a giving
> God a visit: Isa. 26:16, "Lord, in trouble have they visited
> thee." The keeping up of this acquaintance is necessary both
> to our present comfort and future acceptance.[19]

Continual prayer is the unexplainable spirit and art of communion with God. It is a means of cultivating a greater bond of
intimacy of union and communion with Christ as we abide in
Him. We may often lack words, but let us never lack heart in
yearning after God's presence and expressing that yearning in the
cries of our hearts. Keep your heart in a praying frame toward God
even when you cannot express your prayers in words.

5. *Work toward organization in prayer.* The apostle Paul prayed constantly for believers and churches all over the world. Paul was a
remarkably busy person, whose life was full of conflicts and trials.
Yet he maintained a system of prayer.

The Puritans would speak of order and "argument" in prayer.
By this, they did not mean a contentious dispute but the use of
ordered reasons by which we petition and plead with God. Stephen
Charnock said, "Arguments may be fetched from those topics so
far as will suit us to plead with God in our case, and there is scarce

---

18. Brooks, *Heaven on Earth,* in *Works,* 2:494.
19. Thomas Manton, *Sermons on Several Texts of Scripture,* in *The Complete
Works of Thomas Manton* (London: James Nisbet, 1872), 17:496.

any of these considerations which have been delivered but may be turned into an argument in prayer."[20] Spurgeon picked up on this theme when he preached an excellent sermon on "Order and Argument in Prayer" in the Metropolitan Tabernacle.[21] Learning this organized method of beseeching God can revolutionize your prayer life if you often find yourself struggling for words or petitions to make.

We can follow these examples by keeping prayer lists and, with God's help, using them to help organize our prayers. At times you will feel more burdened to pray for some than others, but press on even when you do not feel like doing so. John Newton (1725–1827) considered his best friends to be those who prayed for him. Pray through your church directory, dividing the list to cover a reasonable number of people each day. Use other prayer directories to pray through a list of missionaries supported by your church or denomination.

We can also pray through the Ten Commandments, as Martin Luther (1483–1546), would do, and through the Apostles' Creed, and the Lord's Prayer, using each line as a springboard to articulate the cries of our own hearts. The Puritans would also pray through topics of systematic theology, like the attributes of God; and through every facet of Christian ethics, making every general truth particular and personal in each petition we make.

6. *Read the Bible for prayer.* The Puritans would pray through Scripture, citing Scripture and expounding it in their own words. One reason your prayer life may be drooping is that you have neglected

---

20. Charnock, "A Discourse Proving Weak Grace Victorious," in *The Complete Works of Stephen Charnock, B. D.* (Edinburgh: James Nichol, 1865; repr., Edinburgh: Banner of Truth, 2010), 5:252.

21. The proposition of this sermon based on Job 23:3–4 is, "There are two things here set forth as necessary in prayer—*ordering of our cause, and filling our mouth with arguments.*" Charles H. Spurgeon, "Order and Argument in Prayer," in *The Metropolitan Tabernacle Pulpit Sermons* (London: Passmore & Alabaster, 1866), 12:385.

the Holy Scriptures. Prayer is a two-way conversation. We need to listen to God, not just to talk to Him. We do not listen to God by emptying our minds and waiting for a thought to spontaneously come to mind. That's non-Christian mysticism. We listen to God by filling our minds with the Bible because the Bible is God speaking in written form. Our Lord Jesus Christ says in John 15:7, "If ye abide in me, and my words abide in you, ye shall ask what ye will, and it shall be done unto you."

When you read the Bible, do so with the intent of responding to God's Word with prayer. For example, read Ephesians 5 with its many commands for the church and marriage. This is rich material for prayer. Praise God for the love of Christ presented in verses 2 and 25. Turn the commandments into confessions of your transgressions against God's holy law. And bring the laws of God to Him, praying for God to write them on your heart and the hearts of others. Every Scripture passage is fuel for burning prayers.

7. *Keep biblical balance in prayer.* The Puritans would point out how the Scriptures present various kinds of prayer: praise of God's glories, confession of our sins, petition for our needs (spiritual and physical), thanks for God's mercies, intercession for others (family, friends, church, nation, and the world), and our confidence that God is willing and able to answer what we have prayed. We have a tendency to favor some forms of prayer to the neglect of others. For example, you might gravitate toward intercession but neglect thanksgiving. Paul says in Philippians 4:6, "Be careful [or anxious] for nothing; but in every thing by prayer and supplication with thanksgiving let your requests be made known unto God."

Another person might delight in praising God but shy away from confessing sin, forgetting that the apostle John tells us that one mark of walking in the light of God is confession of sins and finding forgiveness from God through the blood of His Son (1 John 1:7–9). Periodically examine your prayers to see if they are

out of balance and give more time and energy to the areas of prayer
you are neglecting.

Taking Hold of God in Prayer

Deep within us, we know that it is impossible to solve prayerlessness by our own strength. The sacredness, gift, and efficacy
of prayer are far above human means. God's grace is necessary
for prayerful praying. Yet grace does not passively wait for God to
strike us with revival. We must seek grace by first seeking the Lord.
David writes in Psalm 25:1, "Unto thee, O LORD, do I lift up my
soul" (see also Pss. 86:4; 143:8). Paul commands us in Colossians
3:1–2, "If ye then be risen with Christ, seek those things which
are above, where Christ sitteth on the right hand of God. Set your
affection on things above, not on things on the earth." Therefore, direct your mind and affections toward our covenant God in
Christ, and draw near to the throne of grace. Just as Jacob wrestled
with the Angel of the Lord and would not let Him go until he was
blessed, so we must grasp hold of God until He blesses us.

Consider three principles for taking hold of God in prayer:

1. *Plead God's promises in prayer.* In His sovereignty, God has bound
Himself by the promises He has made to us. Augustine (354–430)
said that his mother prayed long for his conversion, pleading God's
promises. She "urged upon Thee, as Thine own handwriting," for
God in His covenant mercy chose "to become a debtor by Thy
promises."[22] Psalm 119:25 says, "My soul cleaveth unto the dust:
quicken thou me according to thy word." Thomas Manton, allud-
ing to Augustine, wrote, "One good way to get comfort is to plead
the promise of God in prayer…. Show him his handwriting; God
is tender of his word."[23]

---

22. Augustine, *The Confessions of St. Augustine*, trans. E. B. Pusey (New York:
E. P. Dutton, 1950), 93 [V.ix.17].
23. Manton, *Sermons Upon CXIX. Psalm,* in *Works,* 6:242. Here Manton
quotes Augustine in Latin (cf. *Works,* 7:21).

The Puritans made much of praying God's promises back to Him. John Trapp (1601–1669) wrote, "Promises must be prayed over. God loves to be burdened with, and to be importuned [urgently pressed with requests] in, his own words; to be sued upon his own bond. Prayer is a putting God's promises into suit. And it is no arrogancy nor presumption, to burden God, as it were, with his promise.... Such prayers will be nigh the Lord day and night (1 Kings 8:59), he can as little deny them, as deny himself."[24]

Likewise, William Gurnall wrote, "Prayer is nothing but the promise reversed, or God's Word formed into an argument, and retorted by faith upon God again."[25] He also urged, "Furnish thyself with arguments from the promises to enforce thy prayers, and make them prevalent with God. The promises are the ground of faith, and faith, when strengthened, will make thee fervent, and such fervency ever speeds and returns with victory out of the field of prayer.... The mightier any is in the Word, the more mighty he will be in prayer."[26]

2. Look to the glorious Trinity in prayer. Much prayerlessness in our prayers is due to our thoughtlessness toward God. Our prayers may come from the stress of an immediate need or crisis, or they may become mere habitual talking to ourselves. But God dwells in our prayers most when our minds most dwell on God. Therefore, when you pray, meditate on how the gospel reveals the Father, the Son, and the Holy Spirit to draw sinners to God. Before rushing into your list of requests, bring to mind Scripture texts that speak of the glory of our God, and turn those texts into praise.

Ephesians 2:18 tells us how the three persons of the Trinity operate in our prayers, saying, "For through him [Christ Jesus]

---

24. John Trapp, *A Commentary on the Old and New Testaments*, ed. W. Hugh Martin (London: Richard D. Dickinson, 1867), 1:121 (on Gen. 32:9).

25. William Gurnall, *The Christian in Complete Armour* (1662–1665; repr., Edinburgh: Banner of Truth, 2002), 2:88.

26. Gurnall, *The Christian in Complete Armour*, 2:420–21.

we both have access by one Spirit unto the Father." Prayer is like a golden chain that runs from the Father via the Son and the Spirit back to the Father again. It is decreed by the Father, merited by the Son, shaped into words by the Spirit, and sent back up to the Son, who, through His intercession, presents it as acceptable and pure to His heavenly Father. So lean heavily on the Spirit to help you compose your prayers and trust in Christ to make your prayers effectual. By the Son and the Spirit, your prayers will reach the ears of the God of Sabaoth.

John Owen advised us to commune with each person in the triune God.[27] He did so based on 2 Corinthians 13:14: "The grace of the Lord Jesus Christ, and the love of God, and the communion of the Holy Ghost, be with you all. Amen." So in your prayer life, pursue a deeper and more experiential knowledge of the riches of grace in Christ's person and work, the glory of electing and adopting love of the Father, and the comfort of fellowship with God by the indwelling Holy Spirit. In this way, you will pray not just to receive God's benefits but to receive God Himself.

3. *Believe that God answers prayer.* I fear that we often do not believe in prayer as we should. Psalm 65:2 says, "O thou that hearest prayer, unto thee shall all flesh come." We sincerely come to God only when we believe that He rewards those who seek Him (Heb. 11:6). The Lord Jesus taught that the life of asking is a life of receiving, especially of the graces of the Holy Spirit (Luke 11:9–13). The very nature of God as Father is to give to His children. On the other hand, James rebukes those who ask God for spiritual wisdom to face trials but do not trust Him to give it generously (James 1:2–8).

---

27. John Owen, *Of Communion with God the Father, Son, and Holy Ghost* (1657), in *The Works of John Owen* (1850–1853; repr., Edinburgh: Banner of Truth, 1965–1968), 2:1–274. This excellent book has also been published separately as John Owen, *Communion with the Triune God*, ed. Kelly M. Kapic and Justin Taylor (Wheaton, Ill.: Crossway, 2007).

May we not fall under the verdict of Isaiah 64:7: "There is none that calleth upon thy name, that stirreth up himself to take hold of thee." Instead, we must bestir ourselves to seek the face of the living God!

Be Encouraged to Seek God's Face in Prayer

Prayer is amazing, glorious, delightful work. Yet apart from faith in Christ, prayer is also difficult, demanding, and in many ways impossible. There is not a believer on earth who cannot sympathize with that. So, though I may have bordered on the idealistic in this chapter, my aim is not to discourage you but to encourage you despite your convictions about your own lack of prayer.

I want to conclude with some encouragement: do not despair in your prayer life. Do not expect to become a Daniel in prayer immediately—if ever. Learning to truly pray in our prayers is not just a matter of getting more intentional or focused or methodical in prayer. It involves trials, warfare, and the enabling Spirit of God. Ask God to make you a praying Elijah who knows what it means to battle unbelief and despair, even as you strive to grow in prayer and grateful communion with God. Isn't it interesting that James presents Elijah as someone quite like you and me? He prayed in his praying, but he could also despair in his despairing.

I share these thoughts because idealism can crush us with its incessant and insatiable demands. The Christian life is not just about being hectored for not praying, giving, or witnessing enough. Though we do need to be goaded forward, we must not turn Christianity into legalistic drudgery, with a long list of chores to do each day. In many ways, thankfulness—especially thankful prayer—is often a better motive for everything. If you are a Christian, praise God that you have something invaluable that a non-Christian lacks—you have a place to go with every need and thanksgiving. Thank God for the throne of grace.

Pray for grace to believe and be thankful that God decrees, gives, hears, and answers prayer. If we truly believe these things, we discover the motivation we need to undertake the journey from prayerless to prayerful praying, becoming contemporary Elijahs who, like the Puritans, truly pray in our prayers to our worthy triune God of amazing grace. He is always worthy of being worshiped, feared, and loved—even to all eternity.

Questions for Reflection and Discussion

1. How has this chapter stirred or convicted your heart about your own prayer life (or lack thereof)?

2. One way the Puritans help us with prayer is by keeping prayer rooted in Scripture. How could you incorporate more Scripture in your prayer life?

3. In cultivating our prayer lives we need a combination of spiritual discipline and trusting dependence upon God. This chapter outlined seven ways to take hold of yourself in prayer and three ways to take hold of God in prayer. Which of these practical helps do you need to implement?

9

THE PURITANS
Sustain Us in Suffering with the Sovereign Providence of God

All providences are overruled and ordered for good, according to that blessed promise (Rom. 8:28); not only things that are good in themselves, as ordinances, graces, duties and mercies, but things that are evil in themselves, as temptations, afflictions, and even sins and corruptions, shall turn in the issue to their advantage and benefit…out of the worst of evils God can work good to His people.

—JOHN FLAVEL[1]

In his fascinating book *Brain Rules,* John Medina tells the intriguing story of a woman under the care of the famous British neurologist Oliver Sacks. This older woman, though intelligent and well-spoken, had suffered a massive stroke in the back region of her brain, resulting in her inability to perceive anything to her left. Her perception was limited to the right half of her visual field. Consequently, when she looked in the mirror to put on makeup, she would apply rouge and lipstick only to the right side of her face. At mealtimes she would eat only from the right half of her plate.

---

1. John Flavel, *The Mystery of Providence* (repr., Edinburgh: Banner of Truth, 1995), 198.

Sometimes she would complain to the nurses that they forgot to bring her coffee or dessert or that her portions were too small.[2]

I sometimes find a similar pathology in the spiritual perception of believers. While it is easy for us to recognize God's hand on the right in times of prosperity and blessing, we fail to perceive his hand in adversity on the left. We are grateful for his clear guidance and his gracious provision. But when we are troubled by trials and tribulations, we mistakenly think God has forgotten us, or that He doesn't care, or has turned against us. "Where was God when my wife got cancer?" "Why did I have another miscarriage?" "Why did my child have to die?" "Why didn't God hear my prayers?" These are the perplexing questions struggling saints often ask in the midst of suffering. Even the psalmist cried out, "How long wilt thou forget me, O LORD? forever? how long wilt thou hide thy face from me?" (Ps. 13:1). Like aged Jacob upon hearing the report from his sons that Benjamin must be taken to Egypt, we are prone to look at our circumstances and say, "All these things are against me" (Gen. 42:36), not realizing the truth that even what man intends for evil, God intends for good (Gen. 50:20). Our problem is a truncated understanding of the providence of God. Once again, the Puritans can help us thrive spiritually through directing our trust to God's sovereign providence in the midst of our suffering. In this chapter we will consider the scope of God's providence, the good purposes of God in providence, and our response to God's providence.

The Scope of God's Providence

Let's begin with definitions. How did the Puritans define the providence of God? We find one of the most careful statements in the Westminster Confession of Faith: "God, the great Creator of all things, doth uphold, direct, dispose, and govern all creatures, actions, and things, from the greatest even to the least, by his

---

2. John Medina, *Brain Rules: 12 Principles for Surviving and Thriving at Work, Home, and School* (Seattle, Wash.: Pear Press, 2008), 77.

most wise and holy providence, according to his infallible fore-knowledge and the free and immutable counsel of his own will, to the praise of the glory of his wisdom, power, justice, goodness, and mercy."[3]

This shows the comprehensive scope of God's providential work in the world. In His providence, God upholds, directs, disposes, and governs "all creatures, actions, and things, from the greatest even to the least." Nothing, no matter how seemingly insignificant, falls outside the scope of His will. No corruption, calamity, or crime—no matter how wicked or unwelcome—can thwart His good, gracious, wise, and sovereign purpose.

The best Puritan treatises on God's providence agreed. Obadiah Sedgwick (1600–1658) said, "Divine providence is an external action of God whereby He conserves and governs all things wisely, holily, justly, and powerfully, to the admiration of His own glory."[4] In Part One of *The Mystery of Providence,* John Flavel examined "The Evidence of Providence" in the lives of believers, showing how God's providence governs our birth, upbringing, conversion, employment, family affairs, preservation from evil, and sanctification.[5] Thomas Watson called providence "the queen and governess of the world" and said, "There are three things in providence: God's foreknowing, God's determining, and God's directing all things to their periods and events. Whatever things do work in the

---

3. Westminster Confession of Faith, 5.1. The subsequent sections of this chapter further clarify the relationship between God's providence and second causes; God's use of means (not only His ability to work through them but His freedom "to work without, above, and against them, at his pleasure"); God's ordering and governing of human sin, though without being either "the author or approver of sin"; God's good purposes in leaving His children for a season "to manifold temptations and the corruption of their own hearts"; God's just hardening of the wicked and ungodly; and God's special care and concern, in His providence, for the church.

4. Obadiah Sedgwick, *Providence Handled Practically,* ed. Joel R. Beeke and Kelly Van Wyck (Grand Rapids: Reformation Heritage Books, 2007), 8.

5. Flavel, *The Mystery of Providence,* 27–109.

world, God sets them a working."[6] This is from *All Things for Good,* Watson's helpful treatise on Romans 8:28: "And we know that all things work together for good to them that love God, to them who are the called according to his purpose."

In expounding this verse, Watson said that not only "the best things" (such as God's attributes, promises, and mercies; the graces of the Spirit; the ministry of angels; the intercession of Christ; and the communion and prayers of the saints) work for the good of the godly, but also "the worst things."[7] Among these worst things, Watson included four evils: the evils of affliction, temptation, desertion (God's temporary withdrawal of grace and comfort from the soul), and sin.

Flavel taught the same in *The Mystery of Providence.* For believers, "all providences are overruled and ordered for good, according to that blessed promise (Rom. 8:28); not only things that are good in themselves, as ordinances, graces, duties and mercies, but things that are evil in themselves, as temptations, afflictions, and even sins and corruptions, shall turn in the issue to their advantage and benefit…out of the worst of evils God can work good to His people."[8]

The Puritans were careful theologians and clarified that these evils are not good in and of themselves. Rather, to quote Watson, they are "a fruit of the curse; but though they are naturally evil, yet the wise overruling hand of God [by] disposing and sanctifying of them"[9] uses them for our good. To illustrate this truth, Watson described a watch: "The wheels seem to move contrary to one another, but all carry the motions of the watch: so things that seem to move cross to the godly, yet by the wonderful providence

---

6. Thomas Watson, *All Things for Good* (Edinburgh: Banner of Truth, 2001 repr. of *A Divine Cordial,* 1663), 56.
7. Watson, *All Things for Good,* chs. 1–2.
8. Flavel, *The Mystery of Providence,* 198.
9. Watson, *All Things for Good,* 25.

of God work for their good."[10] Nevertheless, as Sedgwick wrote, "All afflictions take their commission from divine providence. They are not things which come by chance, but by order and appointment."[11]

The "grand reason" all things work together for the good of the saints is "the near and dear interest which God has in His people." Here Watson referred to God's covenant promise to His people, "They shall be my people, and I will be their God" (Jer. 32:38). "By virtue of this compact," Watson wrote, "all things do, and must, work for good to them…. This word, 'Thy God,' is the sweetest word in the Bible, it implies the best relations: and it is impossible there should be these relations between God and His people, and everything not work for their good."[12] These relations, in Watson's exposition, include the relationship of a physician to his patients, a father to his children, a husband to his wife, a friend to his friends, and the head to the members of its body. Through the Lord Jesus Christ, God secures His people in each of these special relationships. He is our Physician, Father, Husband, Friend, and Head, and, as such, He cannot but work for the good of His called and beloved people, His patients, children, bride, friends, and body.

What, then, are God's good purposes in providence—especially in suffering?

The Good Purposes of God in Providence

As Bible people, the Puritans unanimously agreed with the testimony of Romans 8:28 that God works even suffering for the good of those who love him. In their sermons and treatises on God's providential work in and through suffering, they expounded God's good purposes in detail.

---

10. Watson, *All Things for Good,* 25.
11. Sedgwick, *Providence Handled Practically,* 53.
12. Watson, *All Things for Good,* 52.

A notable example is *A Treatise of Affliction* by Thomas Case (1598–1682), now updated by Richard Rushing and published as *When Christians Suffer.* This short book is an exposition and application of Psalm 94:12: "Blessed is the man whom thou chastenest, O LORD, and teachest him out of thy law." Case applied this to "all kinds and degrees of suffering, whether from God, or man, or Satan. Whether sufferings for sin, or sufferings for righteousness sake,"[13] and listed "Twenty-one Lessons which God Usually Teaches His People in a Suffering Condition."[14] Always concerned with application, other Puritan authors drew out similar lessons. We will consider five of God's purposes in afflicting providences.

1. Deeper gratitude for, and moderation in the use of, earthly comfort. "Through sufferings, God teaches us to prize our outward mercies and comforts more, and yet to dote upon them less."[15] Isn't it true that we often fail to appreciate earthly blessings until they have been taken from us? And yet, we are often overly dependent on creature comforts. "Behold, while men fill themselves with the mercies of God, they can neglect the God of their mercies."[16] God's discipline in providentially removing these blessings for a season can both increase our gratitude for them and wean us from inordinate and immoderate use.

Sometimes when people adopt a healthier diet and start eating with more moderation, they become more temperate in their appetites while also enjoying each meal more fully. By eating less, they both decrease their dependence on food and increase their delight in it. The Lord's discipline in our lives works in similar ways.

---

13. Thomas Case, *When Christians Suffer* (Edinburgh: Banner of Truth, 2009), 13.
14. Case, *When Christians Suffer,* 14.
15. Case, *When Christians Suffer,* 15.
16. Case, *When Christians Suffer,* 15.

2. Chastening for, and deeper conviction of, sin. The Puritans regularly emphasized the sinfulness of sin (see chapter 3) and viewed adversity as God's rod for chastening His children and deepening their conviction of sin. Case said, "In affliction God teaches us the sinfulness of sin. Sin is always sinful, but in our prosperity we are not so aware of it. The dust of the world fills our eyes. We don't see clearly the evil that is in sin. In the sharp and bitter waters of affliction God washes out the dust and clears the eyes to discover sin."[17] Though difficult to bear, God's chastening is for our good, confirms our sonship, and leads us to holiness (Heb. 12:5–11).

The Puritans clarified that God's chastening of believers springs not from "vindictive justice" but from "fatherly mercy."[18] When God brings adversity into our lives as discipline for sin, He does this not to satisfy His justice but as a "rebuke and caution, to bring us to mourn for sin committed, and to beware of the like."[19]

> It must always be remembered that, although Christ has borne the punishment of sin, and although God has forgiven the saints for their sins, yet God may God-fatherly correct His people for sin. Christ endured the great shower of wrath, the black and dismal hours of displeasure for sin. That which falls upon us is a sunshine shower, warmth with wet, wet with the warmth of his love to make us fruitful and humble. Christ drank the dregs of that bitter cup, so much of it as would damn us, and left so much for us to drink as would humble us for our sin. That which the believer suffers for sin is not penal, arising from vindictive justice, but medicinal, arising from a fatherly love. It is his medicine, not his punishment; his chastisement, not his sentence; his correction, not his condemnation.[20]

---

17. Case, *When Christians Suffer*, 58.

18. Samuel Bolton, *The True Bounds of Christian Freedom* (Edinburgh: Banner of Truth, 1994), 122.

19. Bolton, *True Bounds of Christian Freedom,* 122.

20. Bolton, *True Bounds of Christian Freedom,* 122–23. Bolton goes on to provide five reasons God chastens his people: (1) for the terror of wicked men, (2) for the manifestation of his justice, (3) to remove scandal, (4) for caution to others,

3. Greater conformity to the character of Christ. Another of God's purposes in suffering is to make us more like His Son, the Lord Jesus. Paul defines God's "purpose" of Romans 8:28 in the next verse: "For whom he did foreknow, he also did predestinate to be conformed to the image of his Son, that he might be the firstborn among many brethren" (Rom. 8:29).

"God's rod is a pencil to draw Christ's image more lively on us,"[21] wrote Watson. One of the most often used images for this in Scripture is the refiner's fire. Remember the words of Peter? Writing to suffering believers about their inheritance, Peter says that they are

> ...Kept by the power of God through faith unto salvation ready to be revealed in the last time. Wherein ye greatly rejoice, though now for a season, if need be, ye are in heaviness through manifold temptations: that the trial of your faith, being much more precious than of gold that perisheth, though it be tried with fire, might be found unto praise and honour and glory at the appearing of Jesus Christ: whom having not seen, ye love; in whom, though now ye see him not, yet believing, ye rejoice with joy unspeakable and full of glory: receiving the end of your faith, even the salvation of your souls. (1 Peter 1:5–9)

As Thomas Case said, "God increases our grace through affliction."[22]

Our gracious Father always has good and gracious purposes in our suffering. He disciplines us that we might share in His holiness and be more closely conformed to the glorious image of Christ. "Oh what owe I to the file, and to the hammer, and to the furnace of my Lord Jesus! who has now let me see how good the wheat of Christ is, that goes through his mill, and his oven, to be

---

and (5) for their own good here, and for the furtherance of their salvation hereafter (*True Bounds,* 123–24).

21. Watson, *All Things for Good,* 28.

22. Case, *When Christians Suffer,* 31.

made bread for his own table. Grace tried is better than grace, and more than grace. It is glory in its infancy."[23]

4. Sweeter and closer communion with God. "Through chastisements, God draws the soul into sweet and near communion with himself."[24] God thus uses suffering to deepen our delight in knowing Him. When we allow "the world to come between God and our hearts,"[25] adversity awakens us to our neglect and contempt of God. "God's people offend most in their lawful comforts because the snare is not so visible as in grosser sins," wrote Case. "While our hearts are warmed with prosperity, we think many times that small sins can do no great harm, but this is a great deception."[26] Case continues,

> The least sin has the nature of sin in it just as the least drop of poison is poison. In smaller sins there is greater contempt for God since we offend him for a trifle, as we count it, and venture his displeasure for a little sensual satisfaction. Great sins deeply wound the conscience and make the soul go bleeding to the throne of grace to mourn and lament, seeking rest for the soul by a fresh sprinkling of the blood of Christ and to recover peace and communion with God. Small sins are swallowed in silence with less regret and unknowingly alienate and estrange the heart from Jesus Christ.[27]

5. Greater longing for heaven. Another of God's purposes in suffering and adversity is to teach us "to prize and long for heaven."[28]

> God by discipline takes our hearts by degrees from this present world and makes us look homeward. He lessens the esteem of the world that we might discover the excellencies

23. Quoted by John Flavel in *The Fountain of Life*, in *Works*, 1:331.
24. Case, *When Christians Suffer*, 29.
25. Case, *When Christians Suffer*, 29.
26. Case, *When Christians Suffer*, 29–30.
27. Case, *When Christians Suffer*, 30.
28. Case, *When Christians Suffer*, 56.

of heavenly comforts and draws out the desire of the soul to
fully desire God's presence. Affliction shows the glories of
heaven: to the weary it is rest; to the banished it is home; to
the scorned it is glory; to the captive it is liberty; to the struggling soul it is conquest; to the conqueror it is a crown of
life; to the hungry it is the hidden manna; to the thirsty it is
the fountain and waters of life, and rivers of pleasure; to the
grieved soul it is fullness of joy; to the mourner it is pleasures
for evermore; to the afflicted soul heaven cannot fail to be
very precious.[29]

Our Response to God's Providence

How should we respond to God's providence in our lives? The
Puritans have much to teach us here. We can summarize their
teaching under two headings: submission and meditation.

Submission

First, we must submit to the will and wisdom of God in ordering
the circumstances of our lives. In the words of Thomas Brooks, "It
is the great duty and concernment of gracious souls to be mute and
silent under the greatest afflictions, the saddest providences, and
the sharpest trial that they meet with in this world."[30] But while it
is our duty to adopt a spirit of resignation, true submission is also
the work of God's Spirit within us. Flavel said, "The duty indeed
is ours, but the power by which alone we perform it is God's; we
act as we are acted upon by the Spirit."[31]

One of the best treatments of submission to God in affliction
is *The Crook in the Lot* by Thomas Boston. This helpful book is
(in part) an exposition and application of Ecclesiastes 7:13: "Consider the work of God: for who can make that straight, which he

---

29. Case, *When Christians Suffer,* 57.
30. Thomas Brooks, *The Mute Christian under the Smarting Rod,* in *The Works
of Thomas Brooks,* ed. Alexander B. Grosart (1861–1867; repr., Edinburgh: Banner
of Truth, 2001), 1:287.
31. Flavel, *The Mystery of Providence,* 211.

hath made crooked?" As Boston reasoned, "A just view of afflicting incidents is altogether necessary to a Christian deportment under them: and that view is to be obtained by faith, not by sense."[32] He expounded this text with three doctrines:

> DOCT. I. Whatsoever crook there is in one's lot, it is of God's making.

> DOCT. II. What God sees meet [fit] to mar, one will not be able to mend in his lot.

> DOCT. III. The considering of the crook in the lot, as the work of God, or of his making, is a proper means to bring one to a Christian deportment under it.[33]

The title of Boston's book needs some explanation. By "the crook in the lot," Boston was not describing "a criminal hiding out on a piece of probably undeveloped real estate!"[34] By "lot," Boston had in mind a person's lot in life, that is, their specific set of circumstances and relations, as determined and ordered by God, "the providentially appointed path that God sets each of His servants to travel."[35] The "crook" in the lot refers to a "piece of adversity" and, particularly, "adversity of some continuance,"[36] that is, the "crooked…uncomfortable, discontenting aspects of a person's life, the things that the Puritans called losses and crosses, and that we speak of as the stones in our shoe, the thorns in our bed, the burrs under the saddle."[37] These adverse and unpleasant aspects of life afflict us all and can touch people in any part of life, including a

---

32. Thomas Boston, *The Crook in the Lot* (Edinburgh: Banner of Truth, 2017), 1.

33. Boston, *The Crook in the Lot*, 3.

34. As J. I. Packer, in his introduction to this classic, rather humorously suggests would be the assumption of many people today. See J. I. Packer, *Puritan Portraits* (Fearn, Scotland: Christian Focus Publications, 2012), 105.

35. Packer, *Puritan Portraits*, 105.

36. Boston, *The Crook in the Lot*, 6.

37. Packer, *Puritan Portraits*, 105.

person's physical capacities and abilities, their calling or station in the world, or their relationships with others.

Concerning domestic relationships, Boston said: "They are in their nature the springs of man's comfort; yet, they often turn the greatest bitterness to him."[38] This may be occasioned by suffering or the loss of a loved one. But "the crook is sometimes made by their proving uncomfortable through the disagreeableness of their temper, disposition, and way."[39] As examples, Boston referred to Job's "undutiful, ill-natured wife (Job 19:17)," Abigail's "surly, ill-tempered husband (1 Sam. 25:25)," Eli's perverse and obstinate sons (1 Sam. 2:25), and Jonathan's furious father (1 Sam. 20:30, 33). "Sin has unhinged the whole creation, and made every relation susceptible of the crook."[40] What diversity we see in human misery!

But, as Boston so clearly demonstrated, these adversities and miseries, these "crooks," are of God's making. "Consider the work of God: for who can make that straight, which he hath made crooked? In the day of prosperity be joyful, but in the day of adversity consider: God also hath set the one over against the other, to the end that man should find nothing after him" (Eccl. 7:13–14). Listen well to Boston:

> It is evident, from the Scripture doctrine of divine providence, that God brings about every man's lot, and all the parts thereof. He sits at the helm of human affairs, and turns them about whithersoever he lists.... There is not anything that befalls us, without his overruling hand. The same providence that brought us out of the womb, brings us to, and fixes us in, the condition and place allotted for us, by him who "hath determined the times and bounds of our habitation" (Acts 17:26). It overrules the smallest and most casual things about

---

38. Boston, *The Crook in the Lot,* 14–15.
39. Boston, *The Crook in the Lot,* 15.
40. Boston, *The Crook in the Lot,* 15. On God's providence in our personal relationships, see also Sedgwick, *Providence Handled Practically,* 77.

us, even the hairs of our head (Matt. 10:29–30). "The lot cast into the lap" (Prov. 16:33). Yea, the free acts of our will, whereby we choose for ourselves, for even "the king's heart is in the hand of the Lord, as the rivers of water" (Prov. 21:1). And the whole steps we make, and which others make in reference to us; for "the way of man is not in himself; it is not in man that walketh to direct his steps" (Jer. 10:23).[41]

Boston went on to show that even with "impure sinful crooks, which, in their own nature, are sins as well as afflictions, defiling as well as grievous," that God "holily permits them," "powerfully bounds them," and "wisely overrules them to some good purpose, becoming the divine perfections."[42] And, therefore, we must submit to God in them. "Since the crook in the lot is of God's making, then, viewing the hand of God in yours, be reconciled to it, and submit under it, whatever it is; I say, viewing the hand of God in it, for otherwise your submission under the crook in your lot cannot be a Christian submission, acceptable to God."[43]

Meditation

Second, we should learn to meditate on the providence of God. This was the main thesis of Flavel's *Mystery of Providence*: "It is the duty of the saints, especially in times of straits, to reflect upon the performances of Providence for them in all the states and through all the stages of their lives."[44] After setting out the evidence of God's providence in the lives of believers, Part Two of Flavel's book shows the reasons, directions, and benefits of such meditation.

Flavel gave four specific directions:

---

41. Boston, *The Crook in the Lot*, 16–17.
42. Boston, *The Crook in the Lot*, 19–21.
43. Boston, *The Crook in the Lot*, 35.
44. Flavel, *The Mystery of Providence*, 20.

- Labour to get as full and thorough a recognition as you are able of the providences of God concerning you from first to last.

- In all your observations of Providence have special respect to that Word of God which is fulfilled and made good to you by them.

- In all your reviews and observations of Providence, be sure that you eye God as the author and orderer of them all (Prov. 3:6).

- Lastly, work up your hearts to those frames, and exercise those affections which the particular providences of God that concern you call for (Eccles. 7:14).[45]

Flavel also warned against abusing the doctrine of God's providence by growing despondent and weary in waiting on the Lord or looking "too curiously into the secrets of Providence," and thus arrogantly attempting to "judge and censure its designs."[46]

With these instructions in place, Flavel devoted a lengthy chapter to expounding ten distinct "advantages of meditating on providence."[47] These advantages include communion with God, the strengthening of one's faith, the experience of inward peace and tranquility, the advancement of personal holiness, and preparation for one's dying hour. "It must needs sweeten a deathbed," Flavel said, "to recount there the several remarkable passages of God's care and love to us from our beginning to that day, to reflect upon the mercies that went along with us all the way, when we are come to the end of it."[48]

Flavel ends his book with an exhortation to his readers to "keep written memorials or journals" of God's providence in their

---

45. Flavel, *The Mystery of Providence,* 117–38.
46. Flavel, *The Mystery of Providence*, 141.
47. Flavel, *The Mystery of Providence*, 143.
48. Flavel, *The Mystery of Providence,* 174.

personal lives, "for their own and others' use and benefit."[49] This is wise advice, as anyone who has benefited from Christian biography knows. How many believers have been helped by reading about God's faithfulness to suffering saints like Calvin, Bunyan, and Spurgeon! One of the ways we can help both ourselves and our families is by recording our experiences of God's faithfulness to us as well.

Flavel himself suffered much. He lost both of his parents to the plague after they were imprisoned in Newgate Prison in 1665. This was after Flavel himself had been ejected from his pulpit in 1662, along with two thousand other Puritan pastors. But perhaps Flavel's greatest suffering was in marriage. In 1655, his first wife, Joan, died while giving birth to their firstborn child. The child also died. Flavel was thus deeply acquainted with suffering when he wrote *The Mystery of Providence* in 1678. By the end of his life, he would be widowed two more times and would have endured all manner of hardship as a persecuted nonconforming minister.

And yet Flavel not only understood but actually embraced God's good and gracious purposes in His mysterious providence. "Many a time have we kissed those troubles at parting which we met with trembling," Flavel wrote.[50] He further stated,

> The Lord does not compute and reckon His seasons of working by our arithmetic.... Out of the worst of evils God can work good to His people.... We cannot understand the mind and heart of God by the things He dispenses with His hand.... The wisdom of God is much seen in the choice of His rods. It is not any kind of trouble that will work upon and purge every sin; but when God chooses for us such afflictions as, like medicine, are suited to the disease the soul labours under, this speaks divine care and love.... Let a Christian, says a late writer, be but two or three years without an affliction, and he is almost good for nothing.... Whatever ends in

---

49. Flavel, *The Mystery of Providence*, 219.
50. Flavel, *The Mystery of Providence,* 169.

the increase of our love to God proceeds from the love of God to us.[51]

Pray God that you will submit more readily to the sovereign providence of God in the sufferings He has ordained for you. He makes no mistakes!

Questions for Reflection and Discussion

1. The Puritans, following Scripture, rightly believed that God providentially governs the full scope of our lives, including both our blessings and trials. How should this shape our perspective on suffering and difficulty in our lives?

2. This chapter outlined five of God's good purposes in providential suffering. Have you discerned some of these purposes at work in your past trials? Can you see specific ways God has used suffering to wean you from the world, chasten you for sin, conform you to Christ's image, draw you into deeper communion with Him, or deepen your longing for heaven?

3. Our response to God's providence should include both submission and meditation. As you seek the Lord in prayer, ask Him to make your heart submissive to His wisdom and to fill your mind with right thoughts about His good providence. If you are struggling through trials, consider reading Boston's *The Crook in the Lot*, Flavel's *Mystery of Providence*, or Watson's *All Things for Good*.

---

51. Flavel, *The Mystery of Providence*, 191, 198, 199, 200–1, 202.

10

THE PURITANS
Search Our Souls with Profound Psychological Insight

[The Puritans] were men of outstanding intellectual power, as well as spiritual insight. In them mental habits fostered by sober scholarship were linked with a flaming zeal for God and a minute acquaintance with the human heart. All their work displays this unique fusion of gifts and graces.

—J. I. PACKER[1]

There is a big difference between knowing there is a problem and knowing how to solve it. This is true in every realm of life, not least the medical.[2]

When my oldest son was ten years old, he became very ill. My wife and I noticed his lethargy, loss of appetite, and increasingly washed-out, sickly appearance. My wife quickly took him to our pediatrician, who diagnosed him with a mild, passing virus. They said he would be better in a few days.

But he wasn't. He was getting worse, so his mother took him in again. They ran a couple of tests, found nothing wrong, and sent

---

1. J. I. Packer, *The Quest for Godliness: The Puritan Vision of the Christian Life* (Wheaton, Ill.: Crossway, 2012), 29.

2. The opening of this chapter has been adapted from the Foreword to John Downame, *The Cure for Unjust Anger* (Grand Rapids: Reformation Heritage Books, 2020).

him home. But by Friday of that week, he was just skin and bones. Our usually extroverted, fun-loving ten-year-old was stuck on the couch with no energy and no appetite, his face more pallid by the day. We were very concerned. My wife called the pediatrician again and, refusing to be put off for the weekend, insisted on bringing him in that afternoon. This time I went with her.

Once again, the pediatrician on call could find nothing wrong. Then she decided to do a urinalysis. After a few minutes, she asked if we had a history of diabetes in the family, then left us again for a few minutes. Naturally alarmed, we started reading about symptoms of diabetes on WebMD. Before the doctor returned, we knew that our son had DKA—diabetic ketoacidosis.

His life was in danger. His pancreas had stopped producing insulin, the hormone necessary for processing carbohydrates and utilizing sugar in the body. His blood sugar and ketones were dangerously high, his blood was acidic, and his internal organs were not functioning properly. The doctor sent us straight to the hospital—and straight to the pediatric unit. "Don't go home, don't collect two hundred dollars," she said. We weren't even to go through registration and admitting. Our son was very, very sick and needed immediate attention.

Next was the short, sobering trip to the hospital; then, several hours of waiting for some assurance that our son would be okay; and finally, a clear diagnosis: Our son had type 1 diabetes. And then we had a crash course on how to manage this disease.

As I write, our son is now seventeen, is managing diabetes well, and is back to his extroverted, enjoyable personality in every way. The Lord was merciful and has used diabetes to help draw him into a deeper dependence on Christ. But our experience reinforced for us a truth that every person must learn: *clear diagnosis is essential for proper treatment.* The reason our son languished with DKA for almost a week was that the doctors and nurses who first saw him misdiagnosed his symptoms. I'm so thankful that my wife's "mom-sense" outweighed their reluctance to see him for that third visit, pushing them to look deeper for the cause of his symptoms.

Clear diagnosis is essential for proper treatment. This is as true in the spiritual life as it is in the physical. For when the maladies of the soul are misdiagnosed, moral mischief and mayhem are sure to follow. Unmortified sin always breeds more sin. Mismanaged soul-care is spiritual malpractice. And this is yet another reason the Puritans are so valuable today.

No other era in the history of Christ's church has left us with a greater wealth of literature on Christian soul-care. The Puritans were pastor-theologians *extraordinaire*. As theologians, they mined the depths of the sacred Scriptures with profound reverence for their divine authority and an earnest desire to elucidate the whole of God's truth for all of God's people. And as pastors, they consistently kept in view the fourfold purpose (or use) for which Scripture was given—namely, "for doctrine, for reproof, for correction, for instruction in righteousness" (2 Tim. 3:16). In J. I. Packer's words, the Puritans "were men of outstanding intellectual power, as well as spiritual insight. In them mental habits fostered by sober scholarship were linked with a flaming zeal for God and a minute acquaintance with the human heart. All their work displays this unique fusion of gifts and graces."[3] Mark Deckard, in a recent book on "the Puritan practice of biblical counseling," says that the Puritans were biblical "psychologists, students of the inner person, before there ever was a field of secular psychology."[4]

In this chapter we turn to another way the Puritans can help fuel our spiritual growth: in the profound spiritual and psychological insight with which their writings search our souls.

---

3. J. I. Packer, *The Quest for Godliness: The Puritan Vision of the Christian Life* (Wheaton, Ill.: Crossway, 2012), 29.

4. Mark Deckard, *Helpful Truth in Past Places: The Puritan Practice of Biblical Counseling* (Fearn, Scotland: Mentor, 2016), 9. For more on the Puritans in relationship to counseling, see Timothy J. Keller, "Puritan Resources for Biblical Counseling," in *Journal of Pastoral Practice* 9, no. 3 (1988): 11–44.

Overcoming Temptation

One of the best examples of this insight is John Owen's short treatise on temptation, which combines mature pastoral experience, keen spiritual perception, and astute psychological insight in giving directions for how to watch against temptation and sin, all the while pointing us to the riches of the gospel for our protection and defense. Written on the basis of Matthew 26:41, "Watch and pray, that ye enter not into temptation," Owen considers three things in Christ's words:

1. The *evil* cautioned against—*temptation*
2. The *means* by which it prevails—by our *entering into it*
3. The *way* of preventing it—*watch* and *pray*[5]

Owen begins by considering the general nature of testing and describing the nature of temptation. "A temptation," he writes, "is anything that, for any reason, exerts a force or influence to seduce and draw the mind and heart of man from the obedience which God requires of him into any kind of sin."[6] This is the evil against which Jesus cautioned His disciples with the exhortation to "watch and pray."[7]

Owen distinguishes "entering into temptation" from merely being tempted.[8] Believers are never wholly free from temptation during their earthly sojourns, yet our Lord exhorts us to watch and pray lest we "enter into temptation" (Matt. 28:41; Luke 22:46). What then does it mean to enter into temptation? Owen describes the experience: "All will experience a season in which their temptations will be more urgent, sin's reasonings more plausible, its

---

5. John Owen, *Temptation Resisted and Repulsed: Abridged and made easy to read by Richard Rushing* (Edinburgh: Banner of Truth, 2007), 3.

6. Owen, *Temptation Resisted and Repulsed,* 10.

7. For more on the Puritan practice of watching, see Brian G. Hedges, *Watchfulness: Recovering a Lost Spiritual Discipline* (Grand Rapids: Reformation Heritage Books, 2018).

8. Owen, *Temptation Resisted and Repulsed,* 12.

pretensions more glorious, hopes of recovery seemingly clearer, opportunities broader and more open, the doors of evil more beautiful than ever they have been before."[9]

A person knows they have entered into temptation when: (1) they are "drawn into sin,"[10] (2) the temptations come with "great violence,"[11] (3) "the heart begins secretly to enjoy the matter of the temptation,"[12] (4) their circumstances in life provide an opportunity for "lust to be stirred up and provoked,"[13] and (5) they "become weak, negligent or formal" in spiritual duties, thus contenting themselves with "careless, lifeless performance of them, without delight, joy, or satisfaction" to the soul.[14] "This is a certain rule," Owen writes, going on:

> If a man's heart grows cold, negligent, or formal in his duties and in the worship of God, either as to the matter or the manner of them, and this is different from his former manner, then one temptation or other has laid hold upon him. The world, pride, uncleanness, self-seeking, malice, envy or one thing or another has possessed his spirit.... As it is in the sickness of the body, if a man finds his spirit faint, his heart oppressed, or his head heavy, the whole person is affected, and even if he does not have a temperature, yet he will cry, "I fear I am getting a fever, I am so out of order and unwell." A man may do so also in the sickness of the soul. If he finds his pulse is not beating properly and evenly towards his duties of worship and communion with God, if his spirit is low, and his heart fainting, let him conclude that, though his lust does not yet burn or rage within him, he has entered into temptation.[15]

9. Owen, *Temptation Resisted and Repulsed,* 15.
10. Owen, *Temptation Resisted and Repulsed,* 52.
11. Owen, *Temptation Resisted and Repulsed,* 53.
12. Owen, *Temptation Resisted and Repulsed,* 54.
13. Owen, *Temptation Resisted and Repulsed,* 56.
14. Owen, *Temptation Resisted and Repulsed,* 58.
15. Owen, *Temptation Resisted and Repulsed,* 59.

How, then, are we to fortify ourselves against entering into temptation? The answer, summarized in the words of our Lord, is "watch and pray." The second half of Owen's book is an extended meditation and application of this twofold command, broken down into numerous practical observations, insights, and directions. Here is a partial list:

- Always bear in mind the great danger of entering into temptation[16]

- Let no man pretend to fear sin that does not fear temptation also![17]

- Keeping ourselves from entering into temptation is not a thing in our own power. We are to pray that we might be preserved from it because we cannot keep ourselves.[18]

- Let him who would spend little time in temptation spend much time in prayer.[19]

- If you would avoid entering into temptation, labour to know your own heart.[20]

- When you know the tendencies of your heart...watch against every kind of occasion, opportunity, activity, society, solitude, or business that tends to entangle your natural temperament, or that provokes your corruption.[21]

- Be sure to lay up provisions in store against the approach of any temptation…. As for the provision to be laid up, it is what is provided for us in the gospel. Gospel provisions will do this work: that is, they will keep the heart full of a sense of the love of God in Christ. This is the greatest preservative in the world against the power of temptation.[22]

---

16. Owen, *Temptation Resisted and Repulsed*, 61.
17. Owen, *Temptation Resisted and Repulsed*, 62.
18. Owen, *Temptation Resisted and Repulsed*, 64.
19. Owen, *Temptation Resisted and Repulsed*, 67.
20. Owen, *Temptation Resisted and Repulsed*, 77.
21. Owen, *Temptation Resisted and Repulsed*, 79.
22. Owen, *Temptation Resisted and Repulsed*, 80–81.

- Always be alert, so that you may discover your temptations early and recognize them for what they are.[23]

- Meet your temptation at the outset with thoughts of faith concerning Christ on the cross.[24]

- Remember that you are always under the eye of Christ, the great captain of our salvation, who has told us to watch and pray that we enter not into temptation.[25]

As these excerpts show, Owen's book is a potent mixture of deep insight into spiritual experience, bracing warnings against temptation and sin, pointed applications of biblical commands, and a keen understanding of the power of God's grace in Christ to preserve, restore, and sanctify our souls.

Battling Discouragement

Puritan pastors not only helped people deal with temptation but often counseled people in the depths of discouragement, or "melancholy" (their word for depression), and even despair. The causes of depression then, as well as now, were varied, including social, circumstantial, physical, psychological, and spiritual factors. Knowing this, Puritan pastors offered no panaceas. Far from prescribing a one-size-fits-all cure for depression, they delved deeply into both the experience of, and reasons for, different aspects of depression. Then they compassionately applied the full range of Christian doctrine to the specific cases.

In my own struggles with discouragement over the years, I've found the counsel of William Bridge to be helpful over and over again.[26] Bridge wrote a little book for discouraged Christians called

---

23. Owen, *Temptation Resisted and Repulsed*, 84.
24. Owen, *Temptation Resisted and Repulsed*, 86.
25. Owen, *Temptation Resisted and Repulsed*, 117.
26. The following section has been adapted from Brian G. Hedges, *Active Spirituality: Grace and Effort in the Christian Life* (Wapwallopen, Pa.: Shepherd Press, 2014), 63–64.

A Lifting Up for the Downcast. His book is immensely helpful because he addresses different kinds of discouragement so specifically. For example, there are chapters to encourage those discouraged because of suffering and affliction, loss of assurance, a sense of desertion by God, temptation, "weak grace," "great sins," and more. Bridge surveys every conceivable reason a Christian may be discouraged and then skillfully applies the gospel to each case.

For example, sometimes believers are cast down because of their outward afflictions. Under this heading, Bridge includes both "national calamities" and "personal afflictions."[27] And while it is common to feel discouraged when suffering these trials, Bridge argues that "though a man's afflictions be never so great, yet if he be in Christ, and have made his peace with God, he has no reason to be cast down or discouraged, whatever his afflictions be."[28] Bridge presents four broad reasons we should not be discouraged in our trials, considering: "1. What the afflictions and sufferings of the saints are. 2. Whence they proceed. 3. What accompanies them. 4. What follows them, and what is wrought by them."[29] The advice that follows is a masterful amalgam of compassionate argument, striking illustration, and gospel truth. Bridge reasons, "If all the sufferings of God's people come from divine love, the love of God in Christ to them, then have they no reason to be discouraged though they be much afflicted. Every rod is a rosemary to them, fruits of their Father's love."[30]

Bridge also notes that "affliction is God's soap. Before a godly man goes into afflictions, his very graces are mixed with sin. His faith is mixed and dirtied with unbelief and doubtings, his humility with pride, his zeal with lukewarmness. But now, by his

---

27. William Bridge, *A Lifting Up for the Downcast* (repr., Edinburgh: Banner of Truth, 1990), 192.
28. Bridge, *A Lifting Up for the Downcast,* 193.
29. Bridge, *A Lifting Up for the Downcast,* 193.
30. Bridge, *A Lifting Up for the Downcast,* 195.

tribulation, his garments and robes are made white, and washed, and he shall be of a more royal spirit, and be clothed with robes."[31]

Bridge also counsels those who are discouraged by their own sins. While he is clear that "the sins of God's own people do grieve the Spirit of God, are a dishonor to Jesus Christ, and do wound the name of God, and the profession of Christ,"[32] Bridge still insists that "saints have no reason to be discouraged or cast down."[33]

Why? Because saints know that "they shall never be condemned for their sin, whatever it be."[34] Further, their sins cannot separate them from God. Bridge is really helpful here: "Their sins may cause a strangeness between God and them, but shall never cause an enmity. Their sins may hide God's face from them, but shall never turn God's back upon them. Those whom God loves, He loves unto the end."[35]

Furthermore, Christians shouldn't be discouraged because "the overruling hand of grace" can turn even their sins into an "occasion of more grace and comfort.... God never permits His people to fall into any sin but He intends to make that sin an inlet into further grace and comfort for them."[36]

Of course, there is an appropriate kind of sorrow that leads to repentance, but this is sorrow marked by humble trust in the Lord, not fretful discouragement or fearful despair. Bridge helpfully distinguishes discouragement from true humility: "When a man is humbled, truly humbled, the object of his grief or sorrow or trouble is sin itself, as a dishonor done unto God. The object of discouragement is a man's own condition."[37]

Discouragement, in other words, is ultimately self-centered rather than God-centered. And when we are focused on ourselves,

31. Bridge, *A Lifting Up for the Downcast*, 208.
32. Bridge, *A Lifting Up for the Downcast*, 69.
33. Bridge, *A Lifting Up for the Downcast*, 69.
34. Bridge, *A Lifting Up for the Downcast*, 69.
35. Bridge, *A Lifting Up for the Downcast*, 70.
36. Bridge, *A Lifting Up for the Downcast*, 71.
37. Bridge, *A Lifting Up for the Downcast*, 81.

we will lack joy. This is a radical but helpful insight! Bridge goes on to say that "true humiliation is no enemy but a real friend unto spiritual joy, to our rejoicing in God. The more a man is humbled for sin committed, the more he will rejoice in God, and rejoice that he can grieve for sin."[38] According to Bridge, this holds true even in the case of great sins. We should *always* be humbled, but *never* discouraged: "A man is to be humbled for his sin, although it be never so small, but he is not to be discouraged for his sin, though it never be so great."[39]

These important distinctions correspond to Paul's distinction between godly and worldly sorrow in 2 Corinthians 7. Godly sorrow gives birth to repentance, while the sorrow of the world spawns death. It is crucial for us to guard ourselves from the latter, for it is easy for us to become discouraged about specific sins, while not really being repentant at all. Discouragement is often just the flipside of self-confidence. I recall reading somewhere that "to be disappointed in yourself is to have believed in yourself." We must learn to guard against both that kind of discouragement and the self-confidence that inevitably leads to it. Instead, we must keep our eyes steadfastly on God and His sustaining and sanctifying grace. Only His grace can preserve us from falling in the first place. And only His grace can restore us after we have sinned.

Learning Contentment

The Puritans also provided helpful guidance on the nature and development of Christian contentment. Living as we do in a time of unparalleled consumerism, the need for contentment could not be greater. The ubiquitous prevalence of social media has exacerbated our temptations to envy, anxiety, and discontentment.

For a wonderful antidote to these temptations, we turn to *The Rare Jewel of Christian Contentment* by Jeremiah Burroughs. The thesis of Burroughs's book is "that to be well skilled in the

---

38. Bridge, *A Lifting Up for the Downcast,* 82.
39. Bridge, *A Lifting Up for the Downcast,* 83.

mystery of Christian contentment is the duty, glory and excellence of a Christian."[40] He expounds Christian contentment under four headings:

1. The nature of Christian contentment: what it is

2. The art and mystery of it

3. What lessons must be learned to bring the heart to contentment

4. Wherein the glorious excellence of this grace chiefly consists[41]

In typical Puritan form, Burroughs begins with a thorough definition: "Christian contentment is that sweet, inward, quiet, gracious frame of spirit, which freely submits to and delights in God's wise and fatherly disposal in every condition."[42]

Burroughs's book, a reflection on Paul's words from Philippians 4:11 ("I have learned in whatsoever state I am, therewith to be content"), probes deep into the nature of contentment, showing that it is both: (1) a grace, wrought in our hearts by the work of God's Spirit, and (2) a practical skill that must be learned. This twofold approach strikes a wonderful biblical balance. Let's consider each in turn.

First, Burroughs emphasizes the inward and gracious character of true contentment. "Contentment is a sweet, *inward,* heart-thing," he writes. "It is a work of the Spirit indoors."[43] By showing that contentment is a gracious disposition of the heart, Burroughs steers us away from both externalism and self-trust. Contentment

---

40. Jeremiah Burroughs, *The Rare Jewel of Christian Contentment* (Edinburgh: Banner of Truth, 1981), 19. For further meditation on Burroughs's work, see Sinclair B. Ferguson, *"The Mystery of Providence* by John Flavel (1628–1691)," in ed. Kelly M. Kapic and Randall C. Gleason, *The Devoted Life: An Invitation to the Puritan Classics* (Downers Grove, Ill.: InterVarsity Press, 2004), 211–24.

41. Burroughs, *Rare Jewel of Christian Contentment,* 19.

42. Burroughs, *Rare Jewel of Christian Contentment,* 19.

43. Burroughs, *Rare Jewel of Christian Contentment,* 20.

is not merely a matter of refraining from complaining outwardly but a genuine quietness of heart. It is "a grace that spreads itself through the whole soul,"[44] including the judgment, thoughts, will, and affections. "Indeed, in contentment there is a compound of all graces."[45] This means that contentment is not merely the result of a naturally quiet temperament, or of pulling ourselves up by the proverbial bootstraps (what Burroughs calls "sturdy resolution"[46]), or of natural reason. True contentment is the fruit of the Spirit's sanctifying work within us, thus requiring a spiritual operation that is greater than bolstered will-power or cognitive-behavioral therapy. It requires the gracious renewal and transformation of our hearts.

But second, contentment is a practical skill to be learned. Paul had to learn contentment, and so do we. The transformation of our hearts does not leave us passive. Burroughs thus shows us how Christ trains us to be content by teaching us the lesson of self-denial, the vanity of the creature, to know the one thing needful, to know one's relation to the world, to see wherein the good of the creature is, to grow in the knowledge of one's own heart, to see the burden of a prosperous condition, to see the evil of being given up to one's desires, to obtain the right knowledge of God's providence.[47]

But this barely scratches the surface of Burroughs's counsel. He also presents fifteen aspects to the mystery of contentment, ten ways in which the excellence of contentment is seen, thirteen evils of a murmuring spirit, ten considerations to content the heart in any afflicted condition, twelve practical directions for attaining contentment—and more! When carefully and prayerfully studied and applied, *The Rare Jewel of Christian Contentment* presents its readers with a thorough spiritual rehabilitation program.[48]

---

44. Burroughs, *Rare Jewel of Christian Contentment*, 26.
45. Burroughs, *Rare Jewel of Christian Contentment*, 29.
46. Burroughs, *Rare Jewel of Christian Contentment*, 29.
47. Burroughs, *Rare Jewel of Christian Contentment*, chs. 5–6.
48. See also Thomas Watson's *The Art of Divine Contentment* (Morgan, Pa.: Soli Deo Gloria, 2001).

Encouraging Pilgrims

One of the most beloved of all Puritan books is John Bunyan's *The Pilgrim's Progress*. Spurgeon reportedly read Bunyan's famous allegory over one hundred times! It certainly repays repeated readings and stands as yet another example of how the Puritans help us with their profound insight into Christian experience. As we conclude this chapter, allow me to share a number of reasons I love and commend this wonderful book.[49]

First, *The Pilgrim's Progress* is a vivid portrait of every true Christian's spiritual journey. Every Christian needs encouragement in their spiritual life. I certainly do, and have often found strength in reading or contemplating Bunyan's masterpiece. I relate to Christian because I am one. Both Christian's victories and failures are very familiar to me. I have carried a burden (of guilt and sin) on my back that could be removed only at the cross of Christ. I have fallen into the Slough of Despond, and I have been pulled out by Help. I have been in Doubting Castle, tormented by Giant Despair, and have found my way out of Giant Despair's dungeon with the key of promise. I have lost my roll[50] through spiritual slothfulness. I have encountered Apollyon's darts as "thick as hail"[51] while in the Valley of Humiliation. And I have found great strength through other believers, just as Christian did.

A second reason I love Bunyan's book is its many rich word pictures. Of course, the entire book is an allegory, but within the story itself there are many striking illustrations of important truths of Scripture. For example, when Christian goes to the Interpreter's house, he sees a very large parlor that is full of dust because it is never swept. Then a man comes in and begins sweeping the room,

---

49. This section is adapted from Brian G. Hedges, "Why We Should Read the Pilgrim's Progress," *The Banner of Truth Magazine*, no. 471 (December 2002): 23–27.

50. The roll was Christian's assurance of salvation. As Bunyan writes, "This roll was the assurance of his life and acceptance at the desired haven." John Bunyan, *The Pilgrim's Progress* (Edinburgh: Banner of Truth, 1997), 44.

51. Bunyan, *The Pilgrim's Progress*, 62.

but his sweeping so stirs up the dust that Christian almost chokes. Then a damsel sprinkles the room with water, "which when she had done was swept and cleansed with pleasure." Christian asks Interpreter, "What means this?" This was Interpreter's answer:

> This *parlour* is the heart of a man that was never sanctified by the sweet grace of the Gospel. The *dust* is his Original Sin and inward Corruptions that have defiled the whole man. He that began to sweep at first is the *Law*; but she that brought water, and did sprinkle it, is the *Gospel*. Now, whereas thou sawest that so soon as the first began to sweep, the dust did so fly about, that the room by him could not be cleansed, but that thou wast almost choked therewith, this is to show thee that the Law, instead of cleansing the heart (by its working) from Sin, doth revive, put strength into, and increase it in the soul, even as it doth discover and forbid it, for it doth not give Power to subdue…[and] even as thou sawest the *Damsel* lay the dust by sprinkling the floor with Water, so is Sin vanquished and subdued and the soul made clean, through the Faith of it, and consequently fit for the King of Glory to inhabit.[52]

This is only one of many such illustrations in Bunyan's classic that help us to better understand biblical doctrine and Christian practice.

Third, this book shows the difference between true and false Christians. In a heart-searching way, Bunyan reveals the difference between a true Christian who struggles and fights against sin and a false professor who manifests no spiritual transformation. One need only survey the many characters Christian encounters to see the difference between the genuine believer and the hypocrite. There are the positive examples of Evangelist, who points Christian to the Wicket Gate (the "strait" gate); and Faithful, who is martyred in Vanity Fair; and the four virtuous women at House Beautiful: Discretion, Prudence, Piety, and Charity.

---

52. Bunyan, *The Pilgrim's Progress*, 26–27.

There are also the negative examples, such as Obstinate, who ridicules Christian for setting out on his pilgrimage to the Celestial City; and Pliable, who decides to join Christian in his journey but is offended at the first sign of trouble (the Slough of Despond) and deserts Christian, never to return. Or consider Talkative, a man who loves to talk about religious things. Yet, as Christian observes, "He talketh of Prayer, of Repentance, of Faith, and of the New Birth; but he knows but only to *talk* of them.... His house is as empty of religion as the white of an egg is of savour."[53] Then there is Ignorance, who believes that he has a well-grounded hope "because his heart tells him so," but when confronted with the fact that "there is none righteous, no, not one," says "I will never believe that my heart is thus bad."[54]

The distinction between genuine Christians and hypocrites is very blurred in people's minds today. If someone has "accepted Jesus," he is considered a "Christian," whether or not there are changes in his life. A person may profess the name of Christ and yet manifest no love for God, no holiness, no interest in the Scriptures, and no yearning for heaven, and still be assured of salvation. Such a person is, in Bunyan's reckoning, no genuine believer but a gospel hypocrite.

The major theme of *The Pilgrim's Progress* is the perseverance of the saints. The doctrine of the perseverance of the saints has been all but lost in the past century. Thankfully, the revived interest in the doctrines of grace and Reformed theology may be turning the tide. But many people have traded the phrase "perseverance of the saints" for the less comprehensive "preservation of the saints" or the half-truth "once saved, always saved." That God preserves His saints is a fully true and very precious doctrine. We are "kept by the power of God through faith unto salvation" (1 Peter 1:5). It is also true that once a person is genuinely saved, such a salvation cannot be lost. The problem with these phrases is not so much

---

53. Bunyan, *The Pilgrim's Progress,* 86–87.
54. Bunyan, *The Pilgrim's Progress,* 168.

what they say as what they do not say. Some people believe that God preserves His people not *from* sin, but actually *in* their sin. And many people now have the notion that "once saved, always saved" simply means that once a person walks the aisle, signs a card, makes a decision, joins the church, is baptized, and/or accepts Christ into their heart, they have a ticket for heaven—regardless of how they live. This is antinomianism. The message of both Bunyan and Scripture is far different.

The Scriptures teach that "he that shall endure unto the end, the same shall be saved" (Matt. 24:13). We are exhorted to "fight the good fight of faith, lay hold on eternal life" (1 Tim. 6:12), and be "followers of them who through faith and patience [perseverance] inherit the promises" (Heb. 6:12). Jesus solemnly declares, "Not every one that saith unto me, Lord, Lord, shall enter into the kingdom of heaven; but he that doeth the will of my Father which is in heaven. Many will say to me in that day, Lord, Lord, have we not prophesied in thy name? and in thy name have cast out devils? and in thy name done many wonderful works? And then will I profess unto them, I never knew you; depart from me, ye that work iniquity" (Matt. 7:21–23). Job affirms that "the righteous also shall hold on his way" (Job 17:9), and Paul unequivocally says that it is those who are reconciled to God who "continue in the faith grounded and settled" and are not "moved away from the hope of the gospel" (Col. 1:23). In other words, only those who persevere in faith and holiness prove that they are truly saved. It is true that none of Christ's sheep will perish (John 10:28). But it is also true that all of Christ's sheep "follow him." *The Pilgrim's Progress* is about the perseverance of a saint. Bunyan might as well have titled his book *The Pilgrim's Perseverance*, for that is its theme.

The story of Christian's dangerous journey illustrates the perseverance of every true Christian. The Christian life is a series of battles that must be fought in the strength of Christ. There will be failures—just as Christian fell into the Slough of Despond, sinfully listened to Mr. Worldly Wiseman, was wounded by Apollyon, and was locked in Doubting Castle. But just as with Bunyan's pilgrim, each obstacle is eventually overcome, and "progress" is made in one's journey to the Celestial City.

A strange scene in the Interpreter's house well illustrates the truth of perseverance. Christian sees "a Fire burning against a wall, and one standing by it, always casting much water upon it, to quench it; yet did the Fire burn higher and hotter."[55] Again he asks the Interpreter, "What means this?" The Interpreter answers: "The Fire is the Work of Grace that is wrought in the heart; he that casts water upon it, to extinguish and put it out, is the *Devil*."[56] Then the Interpreter takes him to the back side of the wall to show him why the fire burns higher and hotter rather than going out. There Christian sees a man with a vessel of oil which he continually, but secretly, casts on the fire. The Interpreter says: "This is *Christ*, who continually with the Oil of his Grace, maintains the work already begun in the heart: by means of which, notwithstanding what the Devil can do, the souls of his people prove gracious still."[57]

What a beautiful picture of God's work to keep us persevering! I hope you will read this wonderful book. Read it more than once. Read it prayerfully and search intently for the rich spiritual lessons it contains. Use it to examine your own heart and to encourage you in your spiritual pilgrimage.

The Puritans and Soul Care

As physicians of the soul, the Puritans are unsurpassed in the history of the Christian church. This chapter has merely scratched the surface of the amazing wealth available to those who are willing to excavate this mine of rich pastoral material. As we conclude this chapter, here are suggestions for how three kinds of readers could benefit from the Puritans.

---

55. Bunyan, *The Pilgrim's Progress*, 29.
56. Bunyan, *The Pilgrim's Progress*, 29.
57. Bunyan, *The Pilgrim's Progress*, 29–30.

First, if you are an *ordinary believer,* you can learn much from the Puritans about "preaching the gospel to yourself."[58] The Puritans were masters of connecting doctrine with duty, truth with practice—but we often struggle to connect the dots between what we believe and how we behave. With the many modernized editions of Puritan books available today, any ordinary believer with the desire to do so, can sit at the feet of some of the best pastors and counselors the church has ever known.[59]

Second, if you are a *professional or lay counselor,* the Puritans can better equip you to wisely care for the souls of others. As Tim Keller observes, "The Puritans had sophisticated diagnostic casebooks containing scores and even hundreds of different personal problems and spiritual conditions."[60] A growing familiarity with these casebooks can provide you with discerning insights into the human heart and refreshing ideas on how to apply gospel truth to specific conditions of the heart.

Third, if you are a *pastor,* the Puritans can help you not only in counseling, but in preaching. Many of their books were originally sermons, and while we would not want to imitate their length, we can learn much from their breadth (in addressing the whole spectrum of human experience), depth (in their penetrating psychological and spiritual insight), and height (in their soaring expressions of worship and devotion to the Lord). Unfortunately, many preachers today tend to be either doctrinal preachers or practical preachers, but not both. It has been said of Jonathan Edwards that "all his doctrine was application and all his application was

---

58. This is now a common phrase in popular Christian writing. It probably comes from D. Martyn Lloyd-Jones, *Spiritual Depression: Its Causes and Cure* (Grand Rapid: Eerdmans, 1965). Lloyd-Jones says, "The main art in the matter of spiritual living is to know how to handle yourself. You have to take yourself in hand, you have to address yourself, preach to yourself, question yourself" (21).

59. See the conclusion of this book for further suggestions on getting started in reading the Puritans.

60. Keller, "Pastoral Resources for Biblical Counseling," 13.

doctrine."[61] Reading Edwards and various Puritan pastors will help you strike this same balance. By skillfully applying the balm of God's word to the wounded hearts of God's people, you will better counsel them from the pulpit.

Questions for Reflection and Discussion

1. Have you struggled with temptation, discouragement, or discontentment? How could you apply the insights from John Owen, William Bridge, and Jeremiah Burroughs shared in this chapter?

2. How do you relate to Christian's journey as depicted in *The Pilgrim's Progress?* If you've never read this great classic, consider doing so now. If you have read it, maybe it's time to pick it up again!

3. How could the Puritans help you to care for your own soul or the souls of others? Read the Conclusion to this book for suggestions on how to begin reading the Puritans.

---

61. Cited in Joel R. Beeke, *Reformed Preaching: Proclaiming God's Word from the Heart of the Preacher to the Heart of His People* (Wheaton, Ill.: Crossway, 2018), 30.

THE PURITANS
Set Our Sights on Eternal Realities

Since your flesh will fail you, you must
mind the salvation of your soul.
—GEORGE SWINNOCK[1]

The Bible speaks in a number of places about "this life" and "the age to come."[2] The *two-worldly* Puritan view of life, which includes both this world and the world to come, is explained at great length in Richard Baxter's first devotional treatise, *The Saint's Everlasting Rest.* This book was a bestseller in Baxter's day, as well as a major contributing factor to the Puritans' meditation on heaven. It was reprinted every year for ten years, despite its size of more than eight hundred pages. It became household reading in many Puritan homes. It was recognized as a first-class statement of what was basic to the Puritan view of life. That same view of life is explored in Bunyan's *The Pilgrim's Progress.*

---

1. George Swinnock, *The Fading of the Flesh and the Flourishing of Faith* (1662; repr., Grand Rapids: Reformation Heritage Books, 2009), 27.
2. See Ps. 17:14; Matt. 12:32; Mark 10:30; Luke 8:14, 18:30, 21:34; 1 Cor. 6:3–4, 15:19; Eph. 1:21; 1 Tim. 4:8; 2 Tim. 2:4; and Heb. 6:5. This section of the chapter has been adapted from my "Puritan Theology Shaped by a Pilgrim Mentality" in Joel R. Beeke and Mark Jones, *A Puritan Theology: Doctrine for Life* (Grand Rapids: Reformation Heritage Books, 2012), 855–57. Used with permission.

Unlike modern Christians, the Puritans believed that you should have heaven "in your eye" the whole time you are walking on earth. For the most part, evangelical Christians today do not live that way—and we are poorer for it. The New Testament is constantly exhorting us to live in two-worldly terms: to keep the hope of heaven before our minds so as to keep our life on earth straight, controlled, and energized. We tend to live more like Epicureans, assuming that this life is all that we have and that what we don't get now we will never get at all. Thus, it is terribly important to us to find fulfillment, contentment, and satisfaction in the here and now. The thought of radical self-denial would make us miserable if we allowed ourselves to take it as our rule for existence.

We are not strong on self-denial these days; we are self-indulgent and spiritually flabby. We do not live in two-worldly terms as the New Testament exhorts us to do and as the Puritans did. They were persuaded that the joys of heaven will make amends for any losses, crosses, strains, and pains that we endure on earth if we follow God faithfully. This outlook was integral to the Puritans. I hope it becomes integral to us today.

The Puritans lived to the full in this life, but as they did so they kept an eye fixed on eternity. Jonathan Edwards wrote, "O God, stamp my eyeballs with eternity!"[3] How much more in our secular age should we cry out, "Stamp eternity, O God, also upon my mind and soul, my hands and feet, and the totality of my being!"

If we would be true pilgrims in this life for God, we must be active pilgrims for the life to come. It is said that some believers are so heavenly-minded that they are of no earthly use. That assessment could not be more wrong with regard to the Puritans, who have shown us that we can be of no earthly use unless we are heavenly-minded. I have often discovered that the more I am focused on future glory, the more zeal I have for the real well-being of

---

3. Gabe Phillips, "Stamp My Eyeballs with Eternity," *Life Changers*, Feb. 24, 2010, http://www.lifechangers.org.za/popular/stamp-my-eyeballs-with-eternity/, accessed June 15, 2010.

those around me. When I visited the puritan-minded Robert Murray M'Cheyne's (1813–1843) church in Dundee, Scotland, and its adjacent cemetery, I noticed a large flat stone that, though weathered, had one word written across it. I got down on my knees to trace with my finger the word: *ETERNITY*. Obviously, the one who placed the stone there wanted every visitor to consider his eternal destiny while walking among the dead.

We are but a heartbeat from eternity, which hangs upon the thin thread of time. Consider that if you have no vision of eternity, you have no understanding of time. Our lives are not just a journey to death; we are either journeying to heaven, that eternal day that knows no sunset, or to hell, the eternal night that knows no sunrise. To which destination are you headed? Are you a follower of Christ Jesus?

The Puritans teach us to live with our sight firmly fixed on eternity. They remind us of the fleeting nature of this life and of the transcendent reality of the life to come and dissuade us from taking a course that would land us in hell while compelling us to pursue earnestly after heaven.

Profiting from Meditation on Death

We all realize that death looms over us as an imminent reality, threatening at every moment to rip our souls from our bodies and launch us into eternity. James admonishes his readers to beware the fleeting nature of this life, imploring us to live wisely in light of the sober reality and conscious expectation of death: "What is your life? It is even a vapour, that appeareth for a little time, and then vanisheth away" (James 4:14). Likewise, Moses prayed, "Teach us to number our days, that we may apply our hearts unto wisdom" (Ps. 90:12). Coming to grips with the limited nature of our time in this world helps us to steward our time and make adequate preparation for eternity. The subject of dying is far from pleasant. But death is coming for us all, and wisdom would have us put our house in order before we are called to give an account for it.

We must not wait until death is at the door to think about it. Dutch theologian Wilhelmus à Brakel (1635–1711) counseled, "Believers ought to know…that it is not only genuinely wise to live in a state of preparation for death, but also that it is a most delightful life. All that is of the world will lose its beauty, the cross will be viewed as soon coming to an end, the conscience will be at peace within, the hope of glory will yield joy, one will actively pursue sanctification, and all will be plain within the heart."[4]

He continued, "Generally, dying will be consistent with the measure in which one has prepared for it…. Therefore, he who desires to have a joyous deathbed ought to be active in spending much time in preparing for death."[5] Richard Baxter observes, "The chief part of our preparation for death [is] in the time of health."[6] The Puritans knew that a person is not ready to live until they are truly ready to die. To live well, we must be prepared to die well.

George Swinnock's *The Fading of the Flesh and the Flourishing of Faith*[7] is a veritable treasure of truths that can bear you up in your darkest hour of trials. In it, Swinnock gives an exposition of Psalm 73:26: "My flesh and my heart faileth: but God is the strength of my heart, and my portion for ever." The doctrines he derives from the text are: "(1) Man's flesh will fail him," which means that death is inevitable; and, "(2) it is the comfort of the Christian, in his saddest condition, that God is his portion," which means that the Lord is a sure solace in the face of death.[8] The treatise expounds on these subjects biblically, theologically, pastorally, and experientially.

In all their thinking on the reality of death and dying, the Puritans did not obsess over it morosely, nor did they view it as an

---

4. Wilhelmus à Brakel, *The Christian's Reasonable Service*, ed. Joel R. Beeke, trans. Bartel Elshout (Grand Rapids: Reformation Heritage Books,1995), 4:312.
5. Brakel, *The Christian's Reasonable Service,* 4:313.
6. Richard Baxter, *The Practical Works of the Rev. Richard Baxter*, ed. William Orme (London: James Duncan, 1830), 4:403.
7. George Swinnock, *The Fading of the Flesh and the Flourishing of Faith* (1662; repr., Grand Rapids: Reformation Heritage Books, 2009).
8. Swinnock, *The Fading of the Flesh*, 11.

ultimate end. Death is the gateway to the life to come. For the believer, death has lost its sting (1 Cor. 15:55). Swinnock gloats that death for the Christian will be "the funeral for all your corruptions and crosses" and "the resurrection of all imaginable delights and comforts."[9] "Friend, if you were prepared, death would be to you a change from a prison to a palace, from sorrows to solace, from pain to pleasure, from heaviness to happiness."[10] "Christians," he ensures, "anchored on the Rock of Ages, are secure in the greatest storm."[11]

It will not fare so well for the unconverted. Swinnock writes, "Whenever death comes, it will be too late to prepare for it."[12] You must prepare today. "Your preparation for death must be now or never. Bees work hard in summer, flying over fields, and sucking flowers, in order to make provision for winter, at which time no honey can be made."[13] Don't put off the preparation for your future provision! "Will you, like a drone [male honeybee], sleep now and starve later? Let your reason judge carefully. Is it a suitable time to prepare your soul for the marriage feast of the Lamb in the dark night of death? What can you possibly hope to do at that dismal hour? The day is gone, and your soul is lost, because you, unworthy wretch, deferred it until it was too late."[14]

This life is but the dressing room for eternity. The bride makes herself ready in this life to meet the Bridegroom when He ushers in the life to come (Rev. 19:7). Yet many foolishly fail to adorn themselves. They are like the uninvited guest who rashly seeks to intrude into glory without a wedding garment (Matt. 22:11–12). Swinnock exclaimed, "How many in our days spend the whole

---

9. Swinnock, *The Fading of the Flesh*, 86.
10. Swinnock, *The Fading of the Flesh*, 56.
11. Swinnock, *The Fading of the Flesh*, 93.
12. Swinnock, *The Fading of the Flesh*, 37.
13. Swinnock, *The Fading of the Flesh*, 38.
14. Swinnock, *The Fading of the Flesh*, 38–39.

forenoon in decking their dying bodies, and leave no time to dress their immortal souls!"[15]

The always-existing and never-ending state of all people in the life to come leads us to consider the eternal realities that eclipse even death itself.

Meditating on Eternal Realities

Eternity for the Puritan meant one of two things: everlasting salvation or irreversible damnation. Swinnock exhorts his readers, in view of heaven and hell, "Since your flesh will fail you, you must mind the salvation of your soul."[16] To prepare properly for death is, in fact, to prepare for nothing less than "the judgment seat of Christ" (Rom. 14:10). William Bates advised, "The consideration of eternal judgment should be a powerful incentive to prepare ourselves for it. The affair is infinitely serious, for it concerns our salvation or damnation for ever."[17]

Preachers used to stress these themes, but for some reason modern evangelicalism has shied away from preaching much about death, judgment, heaven, and hell. Because of the weightiness of these subjects, many people prefer to ignore them. The Puritans remind us that these realities are what is really important. Far from our shunning these subjects, they should occupy our regular and disciplined meditation so as to impact our minds, arouse our affections, and move us to live for eternity.

In his *Treatise Concerning Meditation*, Thomas Watson writes that we should meditate regularly on death, the day of judgment, heaven, and hell. The Puritans had a systematic and detailed method for engaging in biblical meditation. Like a jeweler who pulls out a diamond and holds it up to the light, turning it slowly, so that the reflection and refraction of light can highlight every

---

15. George Swinnock, *The Christian Man's Calling,* in *The Works of George Swinnock* (1868, repr. Edinburgh: Banner of Truth,1992), 1:281.

16. Swinnock, *The Fading of the Flesh,* 27.

17. Bates, *The Everlasting Rest of the Saints in Heaven,* in *Works,* 3:355.

facet, the Puritans would hold biblical truths before their minds' eye and ruminate on them slowly and thoroughly as they appreciated God's creative craftmanship.

Watson described meditation as "a duty wherein consists the essentials of religion, and which nourisheth the very life-blood of it."[18] He described it like this: "Meditation is the chewing upon the truths we have heard: The beasts in the old law that did not chew the cud, were unclean: the Christian that doth not by meditation chew the cud, is to be accounted unclean. Meditation is like the watering of the seed, it makes the fruits of grace to flourish."[19] Clearly he believed that biblical meditation is of great importance as a spiritual discipline and that much benefit can be had from it.

Our purpose here is not to diverge into a consideration of what the Puritans taught concerning meditation but to apply this to our current topic. One of the ways the Puritans set our sights on eternal realities was by teaching us to meditate on those realities. While they excelled at this discipline, modern Christians generally struggle to engage in it, if at all. When was the last time you seriously set aside time to meditate without distraction, in Scripture-based detail, on heaven and hell?

The Terrors of Hell
Watson gets specific in what we should meditate on concerning hell. We should meditate, for one, on "the pain of loss."[20] This is a privative judgment, depriving the sinner of all that is good, the chief of which is the loss of God's favorable presence. Matthew 25:10 says that "the door was shut." Christ shuts the door of opportunity in the face of the damned, and their day of grace is forever over. "To have Christ's face veiled over, and a perpetual eclipse and

---

18. Thomas Watson, *A Christian on the Mount, or a Treatise Concerning Meditation*, in *Discourses on Important and Interesting Subjects, Being the Select Works of the Rev. Thomas Watson* (Edinburgh: Blackie, Fullarton, 1829), 1:197.
19. Watson, *A Christian on the Mount*, in *Select Works*, 1:198.
20. Watson, *A Christian on the Mount*, in *Select Works*, 1:228.

midnight in the soul; to be cast out of God's presence, in whose presence is fulness of joy, this doth accent and embitter the condition of the damned; it is like mingling gall with wormwood."[21]

Likewise, Swinnock ruminates on hell's hopeless eternity: "The sinner's darkest night here has a morning, but his portion there will be darkness forever! There will be no end of his misery and no escape from his tragedy. He will be bound in chains of everlasting darkness, and he will feel the terrors of an eternal death."[22] Darkness conveys hopelessness; it is the divestment of God's good light to be confined to a privation of eternal woe.

The second aspect to meditate on is "the pain of sense."[23] God will positively inflict poor sinners with the fury of His fierce wrath (Rom. 2:5). Watson is not exhaustive in his treatment, but he is articulate. The pain that strikes the senses with sensations of torment is further subdivided into two categories: (1) the place and (2) the company of hell. It is "a place of torment" (Luke 16:28), consisting of "a lake of fire" (Rev. 20:15). The bodies of the damned are forever burned but never consumed by the fire, he says.[24] In the resurrection, their bodies will be reunited with their souls, and in the burning lake, "God's infinite power" will uphold them in the fire without annihilating them.[25]

It is also a place "where their worm dieth not" (Mark 9:44). The worm he understands to be a metaphor for a gnawing conscience. As the worm eats a decomposing carcass, so the "worm" of conscience will eternally eat away at the soul's sense of peace and produce a never-ending torment of despairing guilt. "This never-dying worm Christ speaks of, is the gnawing of a guilty conscience. Melanchthon calls it an hellish fury,—they that will not hear conscience preaching, shall feel conscience gnawing; and so great is

21. Watson, *A Christian on the Mount*, in *Select Works*, 1:228.
22. Swinnock, *The Fading of the Flesh*, 120.
23. Watson, *A Christian on the Mount*, in *Select Works*, 1:228.
24. Watson, *A Christian on the Mount*, in *Select Works*, 1:229.
25. Watson, *A Christian on the Mount*, in *Select Works*, 1:229.

the extremity of these two, the fire which burns, and the worm which bites, that there will follow 'gnashing of teeth,' Matt. 8:12; the damned will gnash their teeth for horror and anguish."[26]

The company of hell is the devil and his angels (Matt. 25:41). Watson writes, "Job complains he was a companion to owls, chap. 30:29. What will it be to be a companion to devils? Consider, 1. Their ghastly deformity, they make hell look blacker. 2. Their deadly antipathy; they are fired with rage against mankind; first they become tempters, then tormentors."[27] When he says that Satan and his hoards become tormentors, he does not mean that they are not also tormented by the fury of God's wrath. He points out a neglected biblical truth that part of the misery of hell will be to have to endure the immediate presence of such a cursed company. The saints will enjoy Christ and His angels, but the damned will know only the company of wicked men and devils.

The Puritans' writings on hell will strike the fear of God into any soul not hardened beyond remedy. There is nothing quite like them in print today. The subject is not pleasant, but it is biblical. When thought upon rightly—not in despair but in the light of the gospel, it is like a bitter medicine; it tastes like poison but has healing effects on the soul. Watson urges, "Meditate much on hell. Let us go into hell by contemplation, that we may not go into hell by condemnation."[28]

With as much as they taught about hell, one may question if the Puritans were imbalanced in their emphases. But if that were the case, did Jesus err in all His many warnings and descriptions concerning hell? The Puritans would point out that they were only following in the steps of the Lord Jesus, who preached more on hell than anyone else in the Bible. Facing eternal reality is not an unhealthy practice; it is the neglect of soberly assessing these realities that lulls souls asleep into a spiritual stupor. A faithful

---

26. Watson, *A Christian on the Mount*, in *Select Works*, 1:229.
27. Watson, *A Christian on the Mount*, in *Select Works*, 1:230.
28. Watson, *A Christian on the Mount*, in *Select Works*, 1:230.

watchman warns of the mortal danger approaching (Ezek. 33:1–9). We need more watchmen today who, like the Puritans, blast the trumpet of God's truth without cowering before the fear of man. How many Christians today have ever studied the horrors of hell in order to "think upon" and "reflect" solemnly, deliberately, intensely, and systematically on the eternal state of those who die apart from saving union with Christ?

Think of how profitable such meditation can be. It would inculcate in us a greater sense of the fear of God, affectionate disdain for the evil of sin, felt awareness of the weight of eternity, awestruck wonder before the divine attributes in their terrifying display of God's vengeance against the damned, a broken heart for a perishing world, urgency to plead with sinners to be reconciled to God, and gratitude for the grace that rescued us from such eternal misery. Who does not need the weight of these truths pressed with greater force upon their lethargic hearts? Watson and other Puritans believed that the neglect of meditating on hell had negative spiritual consequences, even for the believer who by the grace of God will never go there.

While the Puritans excelled in preaching what the Bible teaches about hell without watering down such unpalatable truths, they actually taught and meditated even more on heaven.

The Glories of the World of Love
"Meditation is the life of most other duties; and the view of heaven is the life of meditation," says Richard Baxter.[29] Contemplating the bitterness of hell incited in the Puritans a greater relish for the sweetness of heaven. By way of contrast, as hell is unspeakably horrendous, heaven is ineffably glorious. If hell is privation, heaven is fulfillment and satisfaction. If hell is pure torment, heaven is unmitigated pleasure. If hell is full of the repulsiveness of sin,

---

29. Richard Baxter, *The Saints' Everlasting Rest*, in *Practical Works* (London: James Duncan, 1830), 23:323.

heaven is brimming with the beauty of holiness. If hell is God's wrath, heaven is God's love and favor. If hell is to be tormented by Satan's company forever, heaven is to be ravished with the love of Christ's immediate presence for endless ages.

The Puritans referred to heaven as "a world of love." Love is the queen of Christian graces. When faith and hope give way to sight and satisfaction, love will be perfected and abide forever (1 Cor. 13:13). William Bates said, "Heaven is a world of love, the law of love reigns there: faith and hope shall cease, but love shall reign in heaven: there the saints love God perfectly, and love one another with an invariable affection."[30]

Jonathan Edwards famously described heaven as "a world of love" in his classic *Charity and its Fruits*. Taking up 1 Corinthians 13:8–10 as his text, Edwards proceeds to expound on the doctrine, "Heaven is a world of love." He has six main points, each of which he expounds in turn:

1. The great cause and fountain of love which is there.[31] Heaven is not ultimately about the saints and their love. It is the immediate abode of God's manifest presence in the fullness of His triune glory and blessing. And "God is love" (1 John 4:8). Due to the God-centeredness of heaven, the love that the saints will enjoy is an endless fountain of bliss that is as inexhaustible as the infinite God from whom love flows:

> There dwells God the Father, and so the Son, who are united in infinitely dear and incomprehensible mutual love.... There is the Holy Spirit, the spirit of divine love, in whom the very essence of God, as it were, all flows out or is breathed forth in love, and by whose immediate influence all holy love is shed abroad in the hearts of all the church [cf. Rom. 5:5].

---

30. Bates, *The Everlasting Rest of the Saints in Heaven*, in *Works*, 3:35–36.

31. Jonathan Edwards, *Charity and Its Fruits*, in *Ethical Writings*, ed. Paul Ramsey and John E. Smith, *The Works of Jonathan Edwards* (New Haven; London: Yale University Press, 1989), 8:368.

There in heaven this fountain of love, this eternal three in one, is set open without any obstacle to hinder access to it. There this glorious God is manifested and shines forth in full glory, in beams of love; there the fountain overflows in streams and rivers of love and delight, enough for all to drink at, and to swim in, yea, so as to overflow the world as it were with a deluge of love.[32]

2. *Heaven with regard to the objects of love which it contains.*[33] All of the "objects," or beings and things which are in heaven, are supremely lovely. There is nothing sinful, nothing odious, nothing reprehensible. There is no unlovely person, no false professor, and nothing offensive. There is no deformity or sickness or suffering. All of the objects of heaven are supremely delightful and amiable. The setting, the inhabitants, and the God of heaven are all perfectly lovely. What ravished the souls of the saints on earth as they hoped for heaven will come to be possessed and experienced by them to the full.

3. *The love which is in heaven with regard to the subject.*[34] By the "subject," Edwards refers to the believer's heart. Every heart is impregnated with the love of God to the maximum capacity of what a finite image-bearer of God in Christ can contain. This love flows from the Trinity and encompasses the saints in communion with God.

The infinite essential love of God is, as it were, an infinite and eternal mutual holy energy between the Father and the Son, a pure, holy act whereby the Deity becomes nothing but an infinite and unchangeable act of love, which proceeds from both the Father and the Son. Thus divine love has its seat in the Deity as it is exercised within the Deity, or in God towards himself.

32. Edwards, *Charity and Its Fruits*, in *Works,* 8:369–70.
33. Edwards, *Charity and Its Fruits*, in *Works,* 8:370.
34. Edwards, *Charity and Its Fruits*, in *Works,* 8:373.

But it does not remain in such exercises only, but it flows out in innumerable streams towards all the created inhabitants of heaven; he loves all the angels and saints there.[35]

4. The principle, or the love itself, which fills heaven.[36] Describing this love, Edwards says, "As to its nature, it is altogether holy and divine."[37] Even though there will be differing degrees of rewards by which God graciously blesses the saints, there will be no envy. No one will covet the greater rewards of those of a "higher rank," for they will be made perfectly content in a love that is utterly sanctified. "Most of the love which there is in this world is of an unhallowed nature. But in heaven, the love which has place there is not carnal, but spiritual; not proceeding from corrupt principles, not from selfish motives, and to mean and vile purposes; but there love is a pure flame."[38]

5. The excellent circumstances in which love is enjoyed and expressed in heaven.[39] Edwards explains that, in heaven, love will always be reciprocal, making it truly satisfying to the full.

> Love is always mutual, and the returns are always in due proportion. Love always seeks this. In proportion as any person is beloved, in that proportion his love is desired and prized. And in heaven this inclination or desire of love will never fail of being satisfied. No one person there will ever be grieved that he is slighted by those whom he loves, or that he has not answerable returns. As the saints will love God with an inconceivable ardor of heart, and to the utmost of their capacity; so they will know that he has loved them from eternity, and that he still loves them, and will love them to eternity.[40]

---

35. Edwards, *Charity and Its Fruits*, in *Works*, 8:373.
36. Edwards, *Charity and Its Fruits*, in *Works*, 8:374.
37. Edwards, *Charity and Its Fruits*, in *Works*, 8:374.
38. Edwards, *Charity and Its Fruits*, in *Works*, 8:376.
39. Edwards, *Charity and Its Fruits*, in *Works*, 8:376.
40. Edwards, *Charity and Its Fruits*, in *Works*, 8:377.

There will be no corrupt principle to distort this love, no unseemly imprudence to make it not fitting. Love in its expressions will always be fervent, consummate, and expressed according to wisdom.

6. *The blessed fruits of heaven's holy love.*[41] The first such fruit is perfect behavior and perfect service to God, "without the least sin or failure."[42] The second is perfect peace and joy. Humble love "is a principle of wonderful power to give ineffable quietness and tranquility to the soul. It banishes all disturbance, it sweetly composes and brings rest, it makes all things appear calm and sweet. In that soul where divine love reigns, and is in lively exercise, nothing can raise a storm."[43]

Edwards summarizes it so beautifully:

Love is a sweet principle, especially divine love. It is a spring of sweetness. But here the spring shall become a river, and an ocean. All shall stand about the God of glory, the fountain of love, as it were opening their bosoms to be filled with those effusions of love which are poured forth from thence, as the flowers on the earth in a pleasant spring day open their bosoms to the sun to be filled with his warmth and light, and to flourish in beauty and fragrancy by his rays. Every saint is as a flower in the garden of God, and holy love is the fragrancy and sweet odor which they all send forth, and with which they fill that paradise. Every saint there is as a note in a concert of music which sweetly harmonizes with every other note, and all together employed wholly in praising God and the Lamb; and so all helping one another to their utmost to express their love of the whole society to the glorious Father and Head of it, and [to pour back] love into the fountain of love, whence they are supplied and filled with love and with glory. And thus they will live and thus they will reign in love,

---

41. Edwards, *Charity and Its Fruits*, in *Works,* 8:383.
42. Edwards, *Charity and Its Fruits*, in *Works,* 8:384.
43. Edwards, *Charity and Its Fruits*, in *Works,* 8:384.

and in that godlike joy which is the blessed fruit of it, such as eye hath not seen, nor ear heard, nor hath ever entered into the heart of any in this world to conceive [cf. 1 Cor. 2:9]. And thus they will live and reign forever and ever.[44]

Heaven's hope is not only about the future. It impacts our lives now, in this world. The earnest hope of believers causes them to look to eternity for their reward and not to set their affections on this world. There is a purifying power that hope, by the grace of the Spirit's sanctifying work, effects in the heart. "And every man that hath this hope in him purifieth himself, even as he is pure" (1 John 3:3). The hope of heaven brings the relish and love of heaven's abode to our hearts in this world. In its so doing, temptations are weakened, graces are strengthened, and hope makes us "meet [prepared] for heaven." Our entire life is a preparation in hope, by faith, for the world of love. "O let us be purifying ourselves, and refining ourselves, that we may be made meet for heaven: this should be the end of your hearing, and it is the end of my preaching to you," urged Bates.[45] The contemplation of heaven is a vital aspect to our preparation for heaven.

Do you meditate on heaven regularly? Are you burning with anticipation to behold the King in His beauty? Do the delights of this world seem but trifles to you in view of the delights of the world of love? Are your affections burning so white hot with holy longings after the Father and the Son and the Holy Spirit that you could say with Paul that "to die is gain" because to depart and "to be with Christ" is "far better" (Phil. 1:21, 23)?

---

44. Edwards, *Charity and Its Fruits*, in *Works,* 8:385–86.
45. Bates, *The Everlasting Rest of the Saints in Heaven*, 3:36.

Questions for Reflection and Discussion

1. Do you ever set aside time to intentionally think about the certainty of death, the terrors of hell, and the glories of heaven?

2. Reflect on the vision of "Heaven as a World of Love" as described by Edwards in this chapter. How is this different from your previous ideas about heaven? Do you find Edwards's vision of heaven attractive?

3. How would a greater consciousness of eternal realities change your life?

THE PURITANS
Fill Us with Sacrificial Zeal
for God and His Truth

*Zeal is the fire of the soul.... Every man and woman in the world
is set on fire of hell or of heaven.... Zeal is the running of the soul.
If thou be not zealous for God, thou runnest away after the things of
this world.*

—WILLIAM FENNER[1]

Far from being satisfied with the status quo of a lukewarm Christianity that characterizes the degenerate condition of a languishing
church, the Puritans preached and wrote with great zeal about—
you guessed it—zeal. John Reynolds (1667–1727) published *A
Discourse Concerning Sacred Zeal* in 1716. His words throb with the
vibrant heartbeat of a man consumed with holy zeal who laments
the indifference of (dare I say?) most Christians:

> How long shall we lie still under our formal complaints of
> the decay of Christian piety? How long shall we idly see the
> retirement of warm religion from the hearts and bosoms of
> its professors? Are we willing to yield to all the lukewarm-
> ness and degeneracy that has overspread us? [Even] the truly
> pious are dull and heavy in their religion, [and] march on
> wearily in their appointed race, as if either their Lord had lost

1. William Fenner, *A Treatise of the Affections* (London: A. M. for J. Rothwell,
1650), 132–33.

His glory or His promise to them; or they [have lost] their faith and hope in Him.... Is it not time to proclaim among the churches, the message of the Mediator sent from heaven to the Church of Laodicea: Be zealous and repent?[2]

Like the Laodicean church, too many of us have grown lukewarm. We are not zealous for the things of God. Where today do you find zeal for the honor and glory and holiness of God? Where do you see zeal to cut off the offending hand and pluck out the offending eye? Where is zeal for the advancement of Christ's kingdom, which overcomes all obstacles and perseveres to the end? Our lives are not marked by zeal, nor do they reflect the sacrifices necessary to strengthen and embolden true Christian zeal.

If you have read the Puritans, you may have noticed that their sermons, prayers, and writings encourage believers to "be zealous...and repent," to be "clad with zeal as a cloak," to be "eaten... up" with zeal for the Lord's house and name," and to be "zealous of good works" (Rev. 3:19; Isa. 59:17; Ps. 69:9; John 2:17; Titus 2:14). From their sermons and writings, let us take a look at, first, what zeal is; second, the characteristics of zeal; third, the marks of false zeal; and finally, how to cultivate zeal in our lives today.

What Is Godly Zeal?

William Fenner (1600–1640) wrote, "Zeal is the fire of the soul.... Every man and woman in the world is set on fire of hell or of heaven.... Zeal is the running of the soul. If thou be not zealous for God, thou runnest away after the things of this world."[3]

---

2. John Reynolds, *Zeal a Virtue: or, A Discourse Concerning Sacred Zeal* (London: John Clark, 1716), 1–2. Much of this chapter is abridged and adapted from Joel R. Beeke and Mark Jones, "Puritan Sacrificial Zeal," in *A Puritan Theology: Doctrine for Life* (Grand Rapids: Reformation Heritage Books, 2012), 947–60, which in turn draws from a recently published book, *Living Zealously* (Grand Rapids: Reformation Heritage Books, 2012), co-authored by Joel R. Beeke and James La Belle.

3. Fenner, *A Treatise of the Affections*, 132–33.

John Reynolds defined this zeal as "an earnest desire and concern for all things pertaining to the glory of God and the kingdom of the Lord Jesus among men."[4] You see, zeal is not just one characteristic or attribute. Rather, as Samuel Ward (1577–1640) said, zeal is like varnish, which does not add color but gives gloss and luster to whatever it is applied to.[5] The Puritan John Evans (1680–1730) viewed zeal as a "qualification which should attend us in the exercise of grace, and in the performance of every duty."[6] Fenner wrote, "Zeal is a high strain of all the affections, whereby the heart puts forth all its affections with might."[7]

Ward wrote, "In plain English, zeal is nothing but heat.... It is a spiritual heat wrought in the heart of man by the Holy Ghost, improving the good affections of love, joy, hope, etc., for the best service and furtherance of God's glory."[8] Think of zeal as a flame that brings a pot to a boil—it brings our affections for God's cause to a boil. It enlivens and compels, stirs and empowers, directs and governs us as it sets our affections ablaze for the glory of God and the good of His church. Think of zeal as something that involves every duty and affection in the Christian life. Iain Murray writes, "Zeal instead of being one particular grace is rather a quality which affects every part of the Christian life. The more zeal the more will be the spiritual energy of the Christian in every sense."[9]

This is the type of zeal that is lacking in our churches and hearts today. We may occasionally be zealous, but far too many men, women, and children do not have hearts ablaze for the glory

4. Reynolds, *Discourse*, 18.
5. Samuel Ward, *Sermons and Treatises* (1636; repr., Edinburgh: Banner of Truth, 1996), 72.
6. John Evans, "Christian Zeal," in *Practical Discourses Concerning the Christian Temper: Being Thirty Eight Sermons upon the Principal Heads of Practical Religion*, 7th ed. (London: Ware, Longman, and Johnson, 1773), 2:320.
7. Fenner, *A Treatise of the Affections*, 118.
8. Ward, *Sermons*, 72.
9. Iain H. Murray, "The Puritans on Maintaining Spiritual Zeal," in *Adorning the Doctrine* (London: Westminster Conference, 1995), 75. This chapter is indebted to several insights from Murray's article.

of God. Given the lukewarm temperature of the church today, we could safely assume that most Christians have decided that holy zeal is not necessary. Are you as zealous about God's glory as you are about your reputation? Are you as zealous about communing with the holy Trinity as you are about talking to your friends? Are you as zealous about spiritual fitness as you are about physical fitness? We are zealous about many things but not for the things of God.

The Characteristics of Godly Zeal

Godly zeal is the divine grace that inclines all affections toward God. There are many branches upon which this root bears fruit and many marks that indicate its true nature. These include the following:

1. *God-centered zeal.* Because the author and object of zeal is the living God, the zealous Christian has a fervent love for God and craves His presence. He grieves when God's name suffers injury and is angry when His honor and cause are obstructed. Titus 2:14 says that Christ "gave himself for us, that he might redeem us from all iniquity, and purify unto himself a peculiar people, zealous of good works." Fenner commented, "Thou cannot possibly be one of God's people, if thou be not zealous for God."[10] Zeal is inseparable from love for God because God is so glorious. Richard Baxter wrote, "The nature of holy objects are such, so great and excellent, so transcendent and of unspeakable consequence, that we cannot be sincere in our estimation and seeking of them, without zeal.... To love God without zeal, is not to love him, because it is not a loving him as God."[11]

---

10. Fenner, *A Treatise of the Affections*, 124.
11. Richard Baxter, *A Christian Directory*, in *The Practical Works of Richard Baxter* (repr., Ligonier, Pa.: Soli Deo Gloria, 1990), 1:383.

2. *Biblical zeal.* In contrast to the false zeal for God that Paul refers to in Romans 10:2, sacred zeal is according to knowledge, meaning that it is confined by the rules of Scripture. Thomas Brooks wrote, "Zeal is like a fire: in the chimney it is one of the best servants, but out of the chimney it is one of the worst masters. Zeal kept by knowledge and wisdom, in its proper place, is a choice servant to Christ and saints."[12] True zeal is grounded in the Word of God as the only rule of faith and life. The Pharisees were zealous, but only of private opinions, or party factions, and for unwritten traditions. Christian zeal is ordered by knowledge according to the Word.

3. *Self-reforming zeal.* Thomas Brooks said that zeal "spends itself and its greatest heat principally upon those things that concern a man's self."[13] Of the eight properties of zeal, Richard Greenham began with this mark, saying, "For never can that man be zealous to others, which never knew to be zealous to himself."[14] He explained that "true zeal casts the first stone at ourselves, and plucks the beam out of our own eyes, that we may the better draw the mote out of another's eye. And this is the condemnation of the world, that every man can pry and make a privy search into the wants [lacks] of others, but they account the same wants no wants in themselves.... We call not in our consciences for those things which we dare challenge and cry out for in others."[15]

Beginning with a sincere examination of self is crucial, for it prevents the damnable error of hypocrisy. Greenham said, "It has been a fearful note of hypocrites, and such as have fallen from the living God, that they have waded very deeply into other men's possessions, and gored very bloodily into the consciences of others,

---

12. Thomas Brooks, *The Unsearchable Riches of Christ*, in *The Works of Thomas Brooks* (1861–1867; repr., Edinburgh: Banner of Truth, 2001), 3:54–55.

13. Brooks, *Unsearchable Riches of Christ*, in *Works*, 3:55.

14. Richard Greenham, "Of Zeale," a sermon on Rev. 3:19, in *The Works of that Reverend and Faithful Servant of Jesus Christ M. Richard Greenham* (1599; facsimile repr., New York: Da Capo Press, 1973), 118.

15. Greenham, "Of Zeale," in *Works*, 118.

who never once purged their own unclean sinks at home, nor drew one drop of blood out of their own hearts."[16]

4. *Active zeal*. Having knowledge of God, whom we love, we are zealous in devoting ourselves to the duties required of us in the gospel. We are busy and active, continually involved in holy exploits and executions. Sin deadens the heart to religious operations, for as the apostle says, "When I would do good, evil is present with me" (Rom. 7:21). But, as Brooks notes, "The zealous soul is continually saying to himself, *What shall I render to the Lord?*"[17] The zealous Christian is ready to perform whatever duty God places upon him, certainly to the utmost of his strength, but even above it,[18] whereupon he trusts in the Lord to bring strength out of his weakness and a richness of grace out of his poverty (Phil. 4:13; 2 Cor. 12:9–10). "Christian zeal is not to be confined at home, to our own personal goodness; but has a still wider scope," Evans said. "If it is employed abroad, while our own vineyard is not kept, it is a false pretense, and justly offensive to God and man. But the due exercise of it for our own conduct being presupposed, there is a large field for its exercise."[19]

5. *Consistent zeal*. The bodies of cold-blooded animals take on the temperature of their environment. Warm-blooded animals have bodies that strive to maintain a steady temperature. The zealous Christian is a warm-blooded creature, resisting both the lethargy of cold-heartedness and the fever of fanaticism. Unlike that blind fury that caused Nebuchadnezzar to heat a furnace seven times hotter than normal, the zealous believer is not to be hot by fits,

---

16. Greenham, "Of Zeale," in *Works*, 118.
17. Brooks, *Unsearchable Riches of Christ*, in *Works*, 3:58–59. Cf. 1 Kings 8:18.
18. William Ames, *Conscience with the Power and Cases Thereof* (1639; facsimile repr., Norwood, N.J.: Walter J. Johnson, 1975), 56 (3.6). In this work the pagination is irregular. Therefore, we will cite it also by book and chapter number.
19. Evans, "Christian Zeal," in *Practical Discourses*, 2:330.

nor start out hot only to end up cold (Gal. 3:3), but must keep a continual temperature from beginning to end (Heb. 3:14).[20] He does not yield to faintness or despondency, for even when his flesh is weak and weary his zealous spirit is still willing and active (Mark 14:38). Reynolds quipped, "It may meet with storms, and stones, and stumbling blocks in its way; but its design and temper is to hold on, and march through all to the end."[21]

The Characteristics of False Zeal

Counterfeit zeal may closely resemble authentic zeal, but they differ in important ways. The Puritans would have explained the differences between godly and ungodly zeal in order to train our eye to distinguish the true from the false with sound discernment. One should be cultivated, while the other should be quenched. One is the fruit of piety, the other of carnal passion.

Jonathan Edwards describes godly zeal as the heat that emanates from the sweet flame of love. True zeal is a fervent love for God and neighbor that boils over into all areas of the Christian life, warming all our service to God with a sweetness: "As some are mistaken concerning the nature of true boldness for Christ, so they are concerning Christian zeal. 'Tis indeed a flame, but a sweet one; or rather it is the heat and fervor of a sweet flame. For the flame of which it is the heat, is no other than that of divine love, or Christian charity; which is the sweetest and most benevolent thing that is, or can be, in the heart of man or angel."[22]

In contrast to such sweet love, false zeal can be discerned by a number of its attendant fruits and characteristics.

1. False zeal proceeds not from the flame of sweet love but from the volcano of tumultuous passions. It can be prideful, selfish, envious, divisive,

---

20. Ames, *Conscience*, 57 (3.6); Greenham, "Of Zeale," in *Works*, 116.
21. Reynolds, *Discourse*, 67.
22. Jonathan Edwards, *Religious Affections*, in *The Works of Jonathan Edwards*, ed. John E. Smith (New Haven, Conn.: Yale University Press, 1959), 2:352.

bitter, resentful, even hateful. Rather than warming the affections and enlarging the heart with God's benevolent love, it will consume and destroy and constrict one's affections for Christ's true church. To reference the fruit of the Spirit and the works of the flesh in Galatians 5:19–23, godly zeal sweetly accords with the fruit of the Spirit, while ungodly zeal is tainted by the works of the flesh—especially those works that tend to cloak themselves behind a veil of religiosity.

The Puritans, no strangers to persecution, were very aware that one of the most common ways false zeal has asserted its influence historically is in the persecution of the pious. In the name of serving God, false zeal has assaulted His image-bearers. Richard Sibbes contrasts the love of God that characterizes true zeal from the contempt and evil fruit that accompany false zeal: "Carnal zeal is persecuting zeal, and the persecuting church is the false church. Christ's flock never persecutes wolves. It will not indeed endure to be near them, but it is not cruel against them."[23] The Jewish establishment, exemplified in the ravenous Saul of Tarsus prior to his conversion, was zealous to oppose Christians; in like manner, Rome was zealous to resist the Reformers and their heirs.

John Flavel describes this "blind zeal": "Blind, superstitious zeal, which spends itself only about the externals of religion, usually prepares, and engageth men in a more violent persecution of those that are really godly, and conscientious."[24] Such false zeal burns hot in false religions in their antagonism against Christians all over the world today. This form of false zeal is usually obvious, at least to the genuine Christian, since it is grounded on a false gospel and contradicts Christ's greatest commandment. Yet

---

23. Richard Sibbes, *Exposition of Philippians Chapter 3*, in *The Works of Richard Sibbes* (1862–1865; repr., Edinburgh: Banner of Truth, 1984), 5:79. Similarly, Sibbes said, "There is no true zeal to God's glory but it is joined with true love to men; therefore let men that are violent, injurious, and insolent, never talk of glorifying God so long as they despise poor men." Sibbes, *Works*, 7:187.

24. John Flavel, *Pneumatologia: A Treatise of the Soul of Man*, in *The Works of John Flavel* (1820; repr., Edinburgh: Banner of Truth, 1997), 3:214.

there can be more subtle manifestations of false zeal that are not as immediately obvious.

2. False zeal tends to divorce doctrine from practice. Counterfeit zeal may manifest itself under a guise of piety in the name of upholding sound doctrine. A person may become so zealous for the relatively minor points of their theological distinctives (*adiaphora*: things indifferent) that they harshly criticize, condemn, or disfellowship other sincere Christians for kindly disagreeing with them over the minutia of their theological intricacies. A sectarian or censorious spirit frequents the company of counterfeit religious zeal.

Some Christians today pride themselves in their understanding of Reformed theology or the "Doctrines of Grace," but their knowledge inflates their pride rather than humbling their hearts. The Puritans would warn such a one that simply embracing good theology and being zealous for it is not necessarily a sign of vital godliness. It is possible to be zealous for Reformed theology and yet be unconverted. John Flavel wrote,

> Yea, it is of sad consideration, that amongst many high pretenders to reformation, their zeal, which should nourish the vitals of religion, and maintain their daily work of mortification and communion with God, spends itself in some by-opinion, whilst practical godliness visibly languisheth in their conversations. How many are there that hate doctrinal errors, who yet perish by practical ones? who hate a false doctrine, but, in the mean time, perish by a false heart? It is very difficult to reclaim this sort of men from the error of their way; and thereby save their souls from hell. However, let the means be used, and the success left with God.[25]

While doctrinal compromise and latitudinarian ecumenicalism are great plagues in the modern church, we must be on guard against the misplaced zeal that would tempt us to overreact to this

---

25. Flavel, *Pneumatologia*, in *Works*, 3:214.

downgrade. Our doctrine is no license to mistreat, vex, oppress, or slander fellow Christians. Such carnal zeal can be a real temptation for those who take their theology seriously. Our zealous appreciation for the truth should be tempered with fervent love for Christ's universal church and for our fellow image-bearers. In contending for the truth, let's remember Paul's advice to Timothy: "The servant of the Lord must not strive; but be gentle unto all men, apt to teach, patient, in meekness instructing those that oppose themselves; if God peradventure will give them repentance to the acknowledging of the truth" (2 Tim. 2:24–25).

3. False zeal goes hand in hand with selective obedience rather than wholehearted devotion. The Pharisees were zealous for certain commandments, but they ignored other ones. They strained out gnats and swallowed camels (Matt. 23:24). Religious hypocrisy is characterized by a false zeal that is partial in its obedience to God. One may be zealous in that which is conducive to selfish interests but indifferent toward the weightier matters of God's will that offer no immediate personal benefit. Thomas Watson warned of this in his discourse on *The Upright Man's Character*, where he contrasts Jehu's carnal zeal with Caleb's godly zeal:

> An hypocrite will pick and choose in religion: in some duties he is zealous, in others remiss; "Ye pay tythe of mint, and annise, and cummin, and have omitted the weightier matters of the law, judgment, mercy, and faith," Matt. 23:23. Jehu was zealous against the idolatry of Ahab, but gives a toleration to the golden calves, 2 Kings 10:29. Jehu's obedience was lame on one foot. Some will go over the smooth way of religion, they are for easy duties, but they like not the rugged way of self-denial and mortification: the plough when it comes to a stiff piece of earth, makes a baulk; an upright Christian, with Caleb, follows God fully; Num. 14:24. and where we are so

ingenuous as to do our best, God will be so indulgent as to pass by our worst.[26]

Jehu abhorred Ahab's idolatry and set himself ablaze in the rapid destruction of it. His zeal consumed him, and he could not contain it. "Come with me, and see my zeal for the LORD," he cried (2 Kings 10:16). It was all too convenient for him, for by this means he secured his own kingdom. But when it came time to remove the high places of Jeroboam's golden calves which had long ensnared Israel in apostasy against the covenant, Jehu faltered in his obedience. If he would have removed the calves, he would have provoked the contempt of many in Israel. He thought it would go better with him if he left those idols alone. In the interest of *establishing* his reign, he was zealous to obey; in the interest of *maintaining* his reign, his zeal waxed completely indifferent to the very same sin of idolatry.

Yet, can we honestly say we've never been zealous for some things God commands while being simultaneously negligent of other things? If we would avoid counterfeit zeal, let us be like Caleb, who followed God fully and sincerely, in consistent integrity, with a universal rather than a selective obedience (Num. 14:24)!

4. *False zeal is concerned with external religion but neglects internal grace.* As a Pharisee, Paul boasted of his external privileges and achievements, but his zeal was nothing more than "confidence in the flesh" (Phil. 3:4). People can be zealous for the form of godliness but deny the power of a Spirit-wrought work of grace in the heart (2 Tim. 3:5). Flavel describes the Scribes and the Pharisees: "The form of godliness wards off all convictions; their zeal for the externals of religion secures them against the fears of damnation,

---

26. Thomas Watson, "The Upright Man's Character," in *Discourses on Important and Interesting Subjects, Being the Select Works of the Rev. Thomas Watson* (Edinburgh: Blackie, Fullarton, 1829), 1:333.

whilst in the mean time, their hypocrisy plunges them deeper into hell than others that never made such shews of sanctity and devotion."[27] He says, "Nothing is more common, than to find men hot and zealous against false worship, whilst their hearts are as cold as a stone in the *vitals*, and *essentials* of *true religion*."[28]

False zeal can be spiritually fatal. "No sin entangles the souls of men faster, or damns them with more certainty and aggravation, than the sin of formal hypocrisy; it holds the soul fastest on earth, and sinks it deepest into hell."[29]

What should we do in light of the reality of false zeal? Shunning false fire, we must actively cultivate true fire. If we do not stoke this flame continually, it will surely dwindle and fade out.

How to Cultivate Authentic Zeal

When you look around and see few people who are zealous for the Lord, you may be tempted to dismiss the call to be zealous and settle for something less. Such a response would be grievous to us all, for lukewarmness (Gal. 2:11–13) is as contagious as sacred zeal (2 Cor. 9:2). Real zeal is not beyond the reach of any saints who sincerely ask the Lord for it and diligently give themselves to the faithful use of the means appointed by God to sustain it. For the cultivation of zeal, the Puritans would point us to the means of grace.

The first means to attain Christian zeal is *prayer*. As a *grace* of God, zeal cannot be earned or bargained for but must be given (James 1:17); and as a grace of *God*, it must be asked for by prayer humbly offered in the name of Christ (John 16:23) and received as a gift of the Holy Spirit (Luke 11:13). John Preston (1587–1628) wrote, "The love of God is peculiarly the work of the Holy Ghost…. Therefore, the way to get it is earnestly to pray…. We

---

27. Flavel, *Pneumatologia*, in *Works,* 3:215.
28. Flavel, *Pneumatologia*, in *Works,* 3:216.
29. Flavel, *Pneumatologia*, in *Works,* 3:215.

are no more able to love the Lord than cold water is able to heat itself…so the Holy Ghost must breed that fire of love in us, it must be kindled from heaven, or else we shall never have it."[30]

The second means by which we maintain zeal is *the Word of God*. Ward said, "When [the fire of zeal] is once come down upon your altar, though no water can quench it, yet must it be preserved fresh by ordinary fuel, especially the priest's lips must keep fire alive. Sermons are bellows ordained for this purpose."[31] Preaching the Word is a powerful means to blow on the coals of zeal and keep them aflame because God Himself speaks in preaching. When the Word is faithfully preached, God speaks to our hearts, lighting His match and blowing upon our coals with His Spirit to make our zeal burn afresh. Likewise, the faithful reading of Scripture feeds our zeal by pouring fuel on the holy fire in our bosom. The Word feeds our passion and love for God, which He graciously placed in our hearts.

The third means to maintain our zeal for God is *faithful attendance and fellowship in God's house*. Hebrews 10:24–25 commands us not to neglect the assembly of the saints, saying, "Let us consider one another to provoke unto love and to good works: not forsaking the assembling of ourselves together, as the manner of some is; but exhorting one another: and so much the more, as ye see the day approaching." Fenner wrote, "The coals that lie together in the hearth, you see how they glow and are fired, while the little coals that are fallen off, and lie by, separate from their company, are black without fire. If ever thou desirest to be zealous, make much of the fellowship of the saints."[32]

The fourth means to stir up our zeal for God is *repentance and resistance against sin*. Our Lord Jesus joined zeal and repentance together when He said, "Be zealous therefore, and repent" (Rev.

---

30. John Preston, *The Breastplate of Faith and Love* (1634; facsimile repr., Edinburgh: Banner of Truth, 1979), 2:50.

31. Ward, *Sermons*, 82.

32. Fenner, *A Treatise of the Affections*, 162.

3:19). Our zeal for God is dampened if we refuse to let go of some cherished sin despite the Spirit speaking to our conscience. A hardened heart is a heart cold toward God. If you find yourself growing cold to God, His Word, and His people, then ask yourself if there is some disobedience in your life that you are tolerating despite the warnings of your conscience.

Paul spoke of the renewal of zeal by repentance when he wrote in 2 Corinthians 7:10–11, "For godly sorrow worketh repentance to salvation," and noted, "What carefulness it wrought in you, yea, what clearing of yourselves, yea, what indignation, yea, what fear, yea, what vehement desire, yea, what zeal." Thomas Watson said that zeal is one of "the adjuncts or effects of repentance" and exclaimed, "How does the penitent bestir himself in the business of salvation! How does he take the kingdom of heaven by force (Matt. 11:12)!"[33]

We must remember that seemingly insignificant means are at times God's appointed means and not the ideas and notions of men. And as God's ways and thoughts are far above ours (Isa. 55:8–9), so God's means to Christian zeal will in the end prove to be far above ours, both in simplicity and efficacy.

Pray and Plead for Godly Zeal
Let us conclude with three applications: First, pray for grace to rightly understand the need for Christian zeal. Let us cast away every objection against becoming zealous for God and His glory. Let us see that zeal is essential, first, because it is God's imperative, for He commands us to be "fervent in spirit; serving the Lord" (Rom. 12:11); second, because it accompanies every other Christian grace, such as zealous love and zealous hope; third, because love for the souls of others demands zeal; and finally, because genuine desires for glory demand that we "strive to enter in at the

---

33. Thomas Watson, *The Doctrine of Repentance* (1668; repr., Edinburgh: Banner of Truth, 2002), 93–94.

strait gate" (Luke 13:24) and run to obtain the high prize (1 Cor. 9:24–25).

Second, pray for grace to be motivated rightly for Christian zeal. (1) The zeal of the world for its agenda ought to motivate us to be more zealous for Christ. If the world can be so zealous for causes that will lead sinners to hell, how much more ought Christians to be zealous for the gospel that can lead sinners to everlasting life? (2) The preciousness of time ought to motivate our zeal. How much time have we wasted already? Truly, now is the time when we should double our diligence and be zealous for God. (3) Titus 2:14 teaches us that Christ's redemptive purchase should motivate us, for He "gave himself for us, that he might redeem us from all iniquity, and purify unto himself a peculiar people, zealous of good works." (4) Christ's own example should motivate us. Zeal for His Father so consumed Jesus (John 2:17) that He took every opportunity in public and in private to speak of the salvation that He came to accomplish for His Father. Should we not do likewise? Peter tells us that Christ has left us an example so we might walk in His steps (1 Peter 2:21). If He is aflame with love for souls, with hatred for sin, with compassion for the hurting, with grief for the obstinate, should we not be likewise?

Finally, let us pray for grace to be humbled by our lack of zeal for Christ and His glorious kingdom. May God make us lament our prolonged lukewarmness in religion; may He humble us by showing us how helpless we are to be zealous for Him and how prone we are to embrace sloth. But may He also have mercy on us, hearing our prayers and answering our hearts' longing to be inflamed with holy affections. May He open our ears to hear Christ's intercession for us so that we are fervent in spirit and clothed with zeal as with a cloak. And may God make this holy desire for Christian zeal come to full fruition in us, leading not only to resolutions to be zealous for God henceforth, but also to endeavor to pursue the appointed means to be more zealous for our God.

Questions for Reflection and Discussion

1. Is your life characterized by God-centered, biblical, self-reforming, active, and consistent zeal? What are the evidences of zeal in your life?

2. How do you distinguish between true zeal and false zeal? Why is false zeal dangerous? How do we guard ourselves against it?

3. Think through the four means for cultivating zeal described in this chapter. How can you utilize these four means over the next thirty days? Spend some time praying for the grace to be more zealous for Christ and His kingdom.

Conclusion:
Reading the Puritans

A dwarf must realize his place among giants.[1] This is true of all human achievement. When we survey church history, we discover giants of the faith, such as Aurelius Augustine, Martin Luther, John Calvin, John Owen, and Jonathan Edwards. Amid those giants the Puritans also rise as giants of exegetical ability, intellectual achievement, and profound piety.

Upon this mountain our Reformed "city" is built. We are where we are because of our history, though we are dwarfs on the shoulders of giants. Who would George Whitefield (1714–1770), Charles Hodge (1797–1878), Charles Spurgeon, Herman Bavinck (1854–1921), J. Gresham Machen (1881–1937), or D. Martyn Lloyd-Jones be if not for their predecessors? Despite this, Puritan studies were sorely neglected until the resurgence of Puritan literature in the late 1950s. In some evangelical circles today, Puritan theology is still marginalized, which is their loss. While the Puritans built palaces, we are comfortable building shacks; where they planted fields, we plant but a few flowers; while they turned over

---

1. Cited in Hanina Ben-Menahem and Neil S. Hecht, eds., *Authority, Process and Method: Studies in Jewish Law* (Amsterdam: Hardwood Academic Publishers, 1998), 119. For a varied version of this material, see *Southern Baptist Journal of Theology* 14, 4 (Winter 2010): 20–37. Several parts of this Conclusion have been adapted from other writings by Joel R. Beeke.

every stone in theological reflection, we content ourselves with pebbles; where they aimed for comprehensive depth, we aim for catchy sound bites.

The Latin phrase *tolle lege,* meaning "pick up and read," offers a remedy for this apathy toward spiritual truth. Our ancestors have left us a rich theological and cultural heritage. We can say of the Puritans what Niccolò Machiavelli (1469–1527) said of his evening routine of reading the ancients, "I enter the ancient courts of rulers who have long since died. There I am warmly welcomed, and I feed on the only food I find nourishing."[2]

Returning to Puritan writings will also reward a diligent reader. Whitefield said, "Though dead, by their writings they yet speak: a peculiar unction attends them to this very hour."[3] Whitefield predicted that Puritan writings would be read until the end of time due to their scriptural truth. Spurgeon agreed, saying, "In these [writings] they do live forever. Modern interpreters have not superseded them, nor will they altogether be superseded to the end of time."[4] Today we are witnessing a revival of sorts in reading the Puritans. Initiated largely by the Banner of Truth Trust, which has been systematically and carefully publishing Puritan literature since the late 1950s,[5] Puritan reprints in the last sixty-five years now include nearly two hundred Puritan authors and eight hundred Puritan titles printed by more than eighty publishers. Reformation Heritage Books (RHB) alone—of which the Puritan

2. Cited in *Modern Political Thought: Readings from Machiavelli to Nietzsche,* ed. David Wootton (Indianapolis: Hackett Publishing Company, 1996), 7.

3. George Whitefield, *The Works of the Reverend George Whitefield, M.A....: containing all his sermons and tracts which have been already published: with a select collection of letters* (London: printed for Edward and Charles Dilly, 1771–72), 4:307.

4. Cited in Steven C. Kettler, *Biblical Counsel: Resources for Renewal* (Newark, Del.: Letterman Associates, 1993), 311.

5. Ligon Duncan, in *Calvin for Today,* ed. Joel R. Beeke (Grand Rapids: Reformation Heritage Books, 2010), 231.

line of Soli Deo Gloria is an imprint—sells at discounted prices several hundred Puritan titles that are currently in print.[6]

We are grateful for this resurgence of interest in Puritan writings. In this conclusion, I will consider some ideas on how to begin learning about and reading the Puritans, and then how to continue on in letting the Puritans feed your soul and mature your faith.

Where to Begin Learning About and Reading the Puritans
The sheer amount of Puritan literature being reprinted today and offered online can be intimidating. Furthermore, the number of books written about the Puritans is nearly as vast as the collection of Puritan titles. The Puritan Research Center at Puritan Reformed Theological Seminary alone contains three thousand books of primary and secondary sources, plus nearly five thousand articles about the Puritans.[7]

The Puritans were people of their time, and even while much of what they wrote is timeless, we must understand them within their context. They battled the spirit of their age and waged doctrinal debates pertinent to their day which, at times, seem quite removed from issues of today. Secondary sources help us understand their historical milieu.

The best overall introduction to the worldview of the Puritans is Leland Ryken's *Worldly Saints: The Puritans as They Really Were.*[8] Other somewhat shorter yet helpful introductions include *The Genius of Puritanism* by Peter Lewis, *Who Are the Puritans? And What Do They Teach?* by Erroll Hulse, and *Following God Fully: An Introduction to the Puritans* by Joel Beeke and Michael Reeves.[9]

---

6. www.heritagebooks.org
7. www.puritanseminary.org
8. Leland Ryken, *Worldly Saints: The Puritans as They Really Were* (Grand Rapids: Zondervan, 1990).
9. Peter Lewis, *The Genius of Puritanism* (Grand Rapids: Reformation Heritage Books, 2008); Erroll Hulse, *Who Are the Puritans?* (Darlington, England:

For basic biographies of the Puritans that have been reprinted since the 1950s, together with brief reviews of seven hundred reprinted Puritan titles, see *Meet the Puritans, with a Guide to Modern Reprints* by Joel R. Beeke and Randall J. Pederson.[10] The best way to use *Meet the Puritans* is to read one biography and reviews of that Puritan writer per day, thus using the book as a kind of daily biographical devotional. For short biographies of more obscure Puritans who have not been reprinted since the 1950s, see Benjamin Brook (1776–1848), *The Lives of the Puritans.*[11] For brief biographies of most of the Puritans at the Westminster Assembly, see William S. Barker's *Puritan Profiles.*[12]

For individual studies of various Puritan divines and aspects of their theology, begin with J. I. Packer's *A Quest for Godliness: The Puritan Vision of the Christian Life,* and *Puritan Reformed Spirituality* by Joel R. Beeke.[13] For a more comprehensive book on the theology of the Puritans, covering fifty key areas in which the Puritans expanded on Reformed doctrine especially in making it experiential and practical, showing how they brought doctrine to bear on their daily lives, read *A Puritan Theology: Doctrine for Life* by Joel R. Beeke and Mark Jones.[14]

Another great way to be introduced to the Puritans, is to purchase the Puritan Documentary package produced by Reformation Heritage Books: "Puritan: All of Life to the Glory of God." This

---

Evangelical Press, 2000); Joel Beeke and Michael Reeves, *Following God Fully: An Introduction to the Puritans* (Grand Rapids: Reformation Heritage Books, 2019).

10. Joel R. Beeke and Randall J. Pederson, *Meet the Puritans, with a Guide to Modern Reprints* (Grand Rapids: Reformation Heritage Books, 2006). This book also includes Scottish and Dutch divines whose mindsets are parallel with the English Puritans.

11. Benjamin Brook, *The Lives of the Puritans,* 3 vols. (Pittsburgh: Soli Deo Gloria, 1994).

12. William S. Barker, *Puritan Profiles* (Fearn: Mentor, 1999).

13. Joel R. Beeke, *Puritan Reformed Spirituality* (Darlington, England: Evangelical Press, 2006).

14. Joel R. Beeke and Mark Jones, *A Puritan Theology: Doctrine for Life* (Grand Rapids: Reformation Heritage Books, 2012).

package contains four helpful tools: (1) a 127-minute documentary on the Puritans, with contributions from John MacArthur, John Piper, Sinclair Ferguson, Steve Lawson, and other pastors and theologians from around the world; (2) five discs of thirty-five teaching lessons on the Puritans and Puritan themes by reputable Puritan scholars, covering such topics as the Puritan view of education, marriage, family, politics, preaching, the Sabbath, suffering and sovereignty, work and money; (3) a 280-page workbook on the thirty-five lessons by Joel Beeke and Nick Thompson; and (4) the 175-page book referred to above, *Following God Fully,* that introduces the Puritans and their teachings. The entire package introduces you to the Puritans and their teachings and aims to serve as an "on ramp" to motivate you to get on the "highway" of reading the Puritans.

The Puritans can be difficult to read. Their wording, grammatical structure, and detail can be hard for the modern mind to grasp. Readers unfamiliar with the language of the Puritans might best begin with the relatively new series of shorter Puritan books being published by Reformation Heritage Books under the rubric, "Puritan Treasures for Today." Each one of these titles is short (that is, under 200 pages) and, without sacrificing content, every sentence has been edited so that these books read like they were written yesterday. To date, these titles include Anthony Burgess, *Advancing Christian Unity* and *Faith Seeking Assurance;* William Bridge, *Comfort and Holiness from Christ's Priestly Work;* Jeremiah Burroughs, *Contentment, Prosperity, and God's Glory;* John Flavel, *Triumphing Over Sinful Fear;* William Greenhill, *Stop Loving the World;* John Owen, *Gospel Evidences of Saving Faith* and *Rules for Walking in Fellowship;* Richard Rogers, *Holy Helps for a Godly Life;* George Swinnock, *The Blessed and Boundless God* and *The Fading of the Flesh and The Flourishing of Faith;* and Nathaniel Vincent, *Turn and Live.*[15]

---

15. All of these Reformation Heritage Books titles are available from www.heritagebooks.org

After reading some of the Puritan Treasures for Today—and being amazed at the richness of Puritan writings—you should be ready and eager to read the original Puritan writings. It is best to read short books from some popular Puritan writers before attempting to read Puritans of more theological profundity, such as John Owen and Thomas Goodwin. I recommend beginning with *The Glory of Grace: An Introduction to the Puritans in Their Own Words,* edited by Lewis Allen and Tim Chester, which consists of eleven well-chosen selections of Puritan writings on a variety of important practical subjects.[16] Then, I would recommend beginning with reading the writings of Puritan divines like Thomas Watson, John Flavel, and George Swinnock. Watson writes succinctly, clearly, and simply. His *Art of Divine Contentment, Heaven Taken by Storm,* and *The Doctrine of Repentance* are good places to begin.[17]

Flavel, who was pastor at the seaport of Dartmouth, became known as a seaman's preacher. He is one of the simplest Puritans to read. His *Mystery of Providence* is filled with pastoral and comforting counsel.[18] Swinnock showed a special sensitivity to the Scriptures and could explain doctrines with great wisdom and clarity. Both Flavel and Swinnock have had their entire works published in multivolume sets by Banner of Truth.[19]

The books of Richard Sibbes and Thomas Brooks are also a good place to start, especially Sibbes's *The Bruised Reed* and Brooks's *Precious Remedies Against Satan's Devices.*[20] You may also benefit

---

16. Lewis Allen and Tim Chester, *The Glory of Grace: An Introduction to the Puritans in Their Own Words* (Edinburgh: Banner of Truth, 2019).

17. Thomas Watson, *The Art of Divine Contentment* (Morgan, Penn.: Soli Deo Gloria, 2001); idem, *Heaven Taken By Storm* (Orlando: Northampton Press, 2008); idem, *The Doctrine of Repentance* (Edinburgh: Banner of Truth, 1988).

18. John Flavel, *The Mystery of Providence* (Edinburgh: Banner of Truth, 1963).

19. *The Works of John Flavel,* 6 vols. (repr., London: Banner of Truth Trust, 1968); *The Works of George Swinnock,* 5 vols. (repr., Edinburgh: Banner of Truth, 2002).

20. Richard Sibbes, *The Bruised Reed* (Edinburgh: Banner of Truth, 1998),

from that master of allegory, John Bunyan, though some of his treatises reflect an unexpected intellectual depth from the tinker of Bedford.[21] Then, too, you could move your way through the Banner of Truth's line of Puritan Paperbacks (which is how I began reading the Puritans at age fourteen) or the more recent Pocket Puritans series. Some Puritan titles written by Owen have been abridged by R. J. K. Law and made easier to read. These are good places to start reading the experiential writings of the Puritans.

How to Continue Reading the Puritans

How to proceed next depends on your particular interest. After becoming acquainted with various styles of Puritan literature, you have a broad spectrum of possibilities to consider. What joys you might have wrestling with Owen's weighty treatments of the glory of Christ, his soul-searching treatise on sin, and his exegetical masterpiece on Hebrews! Or how thrilling it would be to ascend the heights of the intellectual and spiritual atmosphere with Jonathan Edwards, or to plumb the depths of divine attributes with Stephen Charnock! You may probe the redemptive glories of the covenant with John Ball (1585–1640) and Samuel Petto (c. 1624–1711) or be allured by the redemptive doctrines of justification and sanctification with Walter Marshall, Peter van Mastricht (1630–1706), or Robert Traill. You could entrust yourself to a competent guide like Edward Fisher (d. 1655) to bring you safely through the law/gospel distinction or be impressed with the profound but simple writings of Hugh Binning (1627–1653). Prepare to be challenged by the soul-penetrating works of Thomas Shepard (1605–1649) and Matthew Mead (1629–1699) or be instructed by the plain reason of Jeremiah Burroughs, Richard Baxter, and George Hammond (c. 1620–1705).

Thomas Brooks, *Precious Remedies Against Satan's Devices* (Edinburgh: Banner of Truth, 1968).

21. *The Works of John Bunyan,* 3 vols. (repr., Edinburgh: Banner of Truth, 2004).

Whatever topic you select, you may be sure that the Puritans have addressed it with scriptural precision, vivid illumination, practical benefit, experiential warmth, and an eye to the glory of God. Many Puritan writings, however, are not for the faint of heart. But the reader who diligently probes Puritan writings with the willingness to gaze under every rock he overturns and prayerfully considers what they say, will be drawn ever more deeply into the revealed mysteries of God. When you follow the writings of these faithful men, you will find that it will be for the betterment of your soul.

Concluding Advice

Where our culture is lacking, the Puritans abounded. J. I. Packer says, "Today, Christians in the West are found to be on the whole passionless, passive, and one fears, prayerless."[22] The Puritans were passionate, zealous, and prayerful. Let us be as the author of Hebrews says, "followers of them who through faith and patience inherit the promises" (6:12). The Puritans demanded a hearing in their own day, and they deserve one today as well. They are spiritual giants upon whose shoulders we should stand.

Their books still praise the Puritans in the gates. Reading the Puritans will keep you on a biblical path theologically, experientially, and practically. As Packer writes, "The Puritans were strongest just where Protestants today are weakest, and their writings can give us more real help than those of any other body of Christian teachers, past or present, since the days of the apostles."[23] I have been reading Christian literature for more than half a century and can freely say that I know of no group of writers in church history that can benefit the mind and soul more than the Puritans. God used their books for my spiritual formation and to help me grow in understanding. They are still teaching me what John the Baptist said,

---

22. Ryken, *Worldly Saints,* xiii.
23. Cited in Hulse, *Reformation & Revival,* 44.

"Christ must increase and I must decrease" (John 3:30)—which is, I believe, a core definition of sanctification.

In his endorsement of *Meet the Puritans*, R.C. Sproul wrote, "The recent revival of interest in and commitment to the truths of Reformed theology is due in large measure to the rediscovery of Puritan literature. The Puritans of old have become the prophets for our time." So, our prayer is that God will inspire you to read Puritan writings. With the Spirit's blessing, they will enrich your life as they open the Scriptures to you, probe your conscience, bare yours sins, lead you to repentance, and conform your life to Christ. By the Spirit's grace, let the Puritans bring you to full assurance of salvation and a lifestyle of gratitude to the triune God for His great salvation.

Finally, consider giving Puritan books to your friends. There is no better gift than a good book. I sometimes wonder what would happen if Christians spent fifteen minutes a day reading Puritan writings. Over a year that would add up to about twenty books, and fifteen hundred books over a lifetime. Who knows how the Holy Spirit might use such a spiritual diet of reading! Would it usher in a worldwide revival? Would it fill the earth with the knowledge of the Lord from sea to sea? That is our prayer. *Tolle lege*—take up and read!